Follow the Child

The Basics,

The Misconceptions,

And Underlying Lessons of a Montessori Education

ROB KEYS

http://keystomontessori.com

ISBN-13: 978-1514215166
ISBN-10: 1514215160

Edited by Shawn Marie Oberrath

Cover Photo by Jay Reiter, jayreiter.com
Cover Design by Robin Ludwig

First printing, July 2015

DEDICATION

for Sandi, Amee, Lij

ACKNOWLEDGMENTS

Most everything good that has happened to me through Montessori education can be traced back to my dear friend and colleague Gary Davidson. I am in debt to him for no less than a career. Lee Anne Robertson and the Cornerstone School were responsible for both the inspiration and time necessary to complete this project. Christine Rainville edited most of this work when it was in column form, battling me on a weekly basis over conjunction use. Selvi Lampman took on the unenviable task of being a first reader and did it marvelously. Shawn Marie Oberrath was the enormously talented copy editor. Corey Ostman was instrumental in every step of the publishing process. And to Bram, Neal, and Sallie, I thank you with all my heart for your enduring friendship.

PROLOGUE

The phrase "follow the child," used in Montessori terms, is an axiom in the truest sense of the word: it is a truth that is self-evident. Upon these three words a pedagogy was built, and this system continues to expand well past the 100th anniversary of its inception. The fact that the world continues to catch up with a model which has been established and successful for more than a century serves as confirmation of its validity. As is the case with so many concepts we encounter in Montessori education, "follow the child" exists as a literal exhortation while at the same time revealing a deeper understanding of child development. Follow the child! As teachers (and good parents), we are exhorted to dictate less information and to allow more exploration. If the child shows an interest in the sensorial materials, the adult gives a lesson! When a child asks, "How do I add these if their denominators aren't the same?," the teacher presents the fraction circles. Follow the interest! Follow the question! Follow the child.

In a larger sense, "follow the child" is also a reflection of two overarching themes. First, the adult's role is one of preparation and guidance and as a facilitator of the natural process that marks each child's development. Second, a strong measure of independence is both a more humane approach to education and a proven component of a more profound level of learning.

Following is riskier than leading. For one thing, you have to watch where you step. For the teacher, this means adopting a level of comfort with trust, yes, but a trust that is buttressed by experience. For the child, being followed also involves trust: trusting that the adult, whether parent or teacher, is there to point things out along the way, provide support in case of a stumble, and allow him or her the space to walk.

◆　◆　◆

Most first impressions of Montessori take place through glass. A parent or student teacher schedules an observation, arrives at the appointed time, receives a badge, a clipboard, and a brief introduction, and then heads down a hallway and stops at the first classroom. Observers have heard of Montessori certainly, from friends or a relative, a magazine article, a blog, a lecture, or a textbook. But to many, that is just like reading the recipe without actually tasting the cake. The observers' scrawled notes afterward are nearly uniform in content:

"I had the great experience of observing a lesson. The children had to display patience and courtesy. They teach so many things through the course of the day."

"Children helping each other with their work. Children do work then pick up and return work once completed. Teachers move around and help children if needed. Self-correcting work."

"Older children helping younger ones."

"Children are all very calm and happy. Classroom is very beautiful and bright. Kids are extremely well behaved."

"I loved that every child was working on 'hands-on' activities."

"I love seeing kids conversing and problem-solving together—not being "shushed." Great cooperation. Lots of imagination."

"Everything with purpose."

"Good room flow. Teamwork and pairing. Routine and organized."

"Teachers kept voices low. Gentle redirection, very good patience."

"So many different activities happening at once. Amid all the activity the kids learn and grow."

"The children's independent play—completing a task and then picking it up and putting it away before starting a new activity. The room felt very quiet, calm (no chaos). The children feel free to move around the room from activity to activity."

"Soft voices, individual projects and small groups. Clean and organized space. Teachers guide by example. Bright and open classrooms. Education everywhere and focus on learning."

"Beautiful classroom!"

To understand a functioning Montessori environment, one must see it in action, with children interacting with Montessori materials and with each other, with direction from Montessori-trained teachers, in a Montessori "prepared environment." In this way, we can think of Montessori as being a dynamic process and, in fact, a dynamic process that is greater than the sum of its parts. If your child is in a Montessori classroom, you will eventually be found out at your neighborhood barbecue, your Thanksgiving get-together, your Christmas party, or elsewhere, having been asked something along the lines of, "So, what's Montessori, anyway?" You will find that it is difficult to describe just one aspect of this pedagogy with any sense of completion. Those beautifully designed manipulative Montessori materials? They are certainly fundamental. The integration and crossover of curricula? Well, sure, they are important, too. The interplay of child, peer, and teacher in a carefully prepared environment? Yes, of course that. The elements of movement, the use of the hand? The nurturing of independence, of self-awareness, of self-control? Yes, yes, and emphatically, yes, they are all essential components! The 3-year age span, the developmentally based presentations, the attention to sensitive periods, the long, uninterrupted work periods? Yes, all of these points contribute to the Montessori pedagogy, but none of these points in isolation will do it justice (we can assume here that the person you've been speaking to at the party has, perhaps, regretted broaching the subject). A Montessori education is all of these things, integrated in play, in harmony, in success and failure, in falling down, in learning from the spill and trying again, and in growth, for children, parents, and teachers alike. To understand Montessori, you have to first look through the glass and then step through the door.

CHAPTER ONE
MONTESSORI MISCONCEPTIONS

A few years back I had a conversation with the head of school at a private school in Cambridge, Massachusetts. His wife, a University of New Hampshire professor, had recently visited our school with about a half-dozen Early Childhood majors. She told her husband that he had to experience this "inspiring place" for himself. Near the morning's end, he remarked that his wife loved the Montessori pedagogy but felt that children should be able to use the materials more creatively. "Ahh, a common Montessori misconception," I explained. Coincidentally, the next day I found a photo of President Obama visiting a Primary Montessori classroom, working with children who had combined the Pink Tower and the Broad Stair in a new, creative way. This is a common, never-discouraged activity in any Montessori Toddler (3- to 6-year-olds) environment. I began to question the origin of this misconception, and others that we all encounter, at parties, at family get-togethers, and in casual conversation, that start with "So your kids go to a Montessori school? That's the one where kids…"

Montessori materials possess two important qualities: self-correction and isolation of difficulty. Therefore, there is a natural, initial use of the material that is presented to the child. The prisms of the Pink Tower and the Broad Stair, for example, are laid out consecutively, from largest to smallest, so the child will experience the discrimination of size and form in gradation. There is an order that underlies the work, allowing the child to discover the logical layout of the blocks or cubes. Seen in this light, the Pink Tower is stacked from the largest cube to the smallest, fulfilling its primary objective, i.e., there is one "right" way. Perhaps it is this singular elegance of the Montessori material that leads to the fallacious idea that "it can only be used in one way." But there is a profound difference between the misuse of a material (not good) and the creative use of a material (good). A piece of the Broad Stair should not be used as a sword, and the Pink Tower cubes should not be crashed together as if they were colliding cars. But at no time is the child discouraged from creative exploration. What happens if I transpose two cubes? Can I build from the smallest cube on the bottom?

The element of choice in a Montessori classroom is worthy of an entire article, chapter, or morning lecture. It is also the root of another common misconception about Montessori, namely, "I heard that kids get to do whatever they want." The genesis of this misunderstanding is obvious. Observation of any Montessori prepared environment reveals happy children independently accessing materials from classroom shelves and working through exercises and activities before replacing them and choosing anew. In fact, one of the strongest components of the Montessori pedagogy is this idea of freedom of choice and spontaneous activity and the profound effect that this has on children's learning. But the Montessori method clearly makes the distinction that this choice is limited to choosing purposeful activity. There is a large distinction between a child engaging in the Stamp Game or participating in a lesson and a child being destructive with the Red Rods or aimlessly wandering around the classroom. In this way, we can say that children in a Montessori environment have freedom of choice as long as they are making the appropriate choices. It may seem Orwellian to state it in these terms, but it is a crucial difference.

The beauty of the environment, the attractiveness of the materials, the matching of activity to developmental stage, all work to guide the child, to entice the child, in choosing appropriate work. In this way, the prepared environment, with the contents of the shelf limited to quality activities, classroom management that encourages a love of learning, and teacher presentations that are impressionistic and engaging, allows us to say to the child, "This classroom is yours. You have the right to work on anything that has been presented to you." Can children "do whatever they like?" Well, no, they cannot. A child misusing a particular material will be guided gently but firmly to a more appropriate usage or to a new material. The aimlessly wandering student will be redirected kindly but purposefully to an activity, or perhaps to a lesson. Further, our expectations for those choices, especially as the child moves through the elementary years, may well include parameters around daily works, such as 30 minutes of math or specific daily writing assignments. In this way, choice is balanced with structure, and freedom is balanced with responsibility.

Do Montessori classrooms "push" children too far too fast? In 1915, San Francisco hosted a World's Fair, entitled "The Panama Pacific International Exposition." An entire assembly line churned out Model T's in 10 minutes flat, and the new transcontinental telephone service connected people who were 3,000 miles apart. At the center of the

Fair, there was a fully operational, glass-enclosed classroom, a model Montessori environment, complete with 30 young students and a teacher. The classroom day ran from 9:00 a.m. to noon and reportedly drew crowds for the duration of its entire, astoundingly long 4-month exhibition. On the Fair's opening day, Dr. Maria Montessori herself gave a Knobbed Cylinder lesson to a student. The students at the Fair, aged 2 1/2 to 6 years old, amazed onlookers with both their academic prowess at such a young age and their comportment in setting up for lunch, dining with silverware and a tablecloth, and diligently cleaning up after themselves. The display garnered immense publicity, and the students (who, at Montessori's insistence, had no schooling background) were dubbed "miracle children." Is this display the root of the idea that "Montessori classrooms push children too far too fast?"

In truth, a core tenet of Montessori pedagogy is the idea of allowing each child to develop at his or her own pace. The "miracle" stories of Montessori children who far exceed traditional expectations for their age level reflect not artificial acceleration but the possibilities that open when children are allowed to learn at their own pace in a prepared environment. In my experience, children shown, in concrete terms, the concept of squaring a two-digit number will invariably want to square a three-digit number, etc. A child shown the various classes of adjectives will question whether other parts of speech are similarly classified. Because it is student centered, the curriculum does not rely on a teacher to be the gatekeeper of new information, new questions, or the next step. Without these limitations, children learn to trust themselves, which often translates into readiness that, sometimes, greatly exceeds their chronological age. Is this a miracle? Well, it is certainly a natural phenomenon. But do you consider the growth of a tomato plant a miracle? The weaving of a spider's web? The laugh of a child? Perhaps "miracle" is exactly the right word to use.

CHAPTER TWO
THE BASICS

Planes of Development

Montessori described human development from birth to adulthood in terms of "planes of development." Each of these planes consists of 6 years, specifically birth to 6, 6 to 12, 12 to 18, and 18 to 24 years. Montessori asserted that each plane of development defined common characteristics of that particular age group. These characteristics, these needs and tendencies, led to the development of the Montessori materials (the manipulative shelf work we see in our classrooms) and inform our decision-making regarding everything from curriculum to the design of the room or "prepared environment."

We can see, then, that Toddler and Primary environments serve the first plane of development, the Lower and Upper Elementary classrooms serve the second plane of development, and the Junior Class marks the beginning of adolescence and the third plane of development. The accuracy in this description is apparent if we look at the greater difference between Primary and Lower Elementary students or between Upper Elementary and Junior students. Conversely, the difference between Lower and Upper Elementary classrooms is much smaller.

Further, Montessori described the planes in broader terms. A strong sense of order marks the first plane. We certainly see this reflected in both the children's activities (sorting, lining up objects, and differentiating items) and the curriculum (sensorial materials and practical life). The second plane is marked as an explosion into the social realm. The methodical 5-year-old morphs into the rambunctious 6-year-old. The Upper and Lower Elementary classrooms meet this need with more group work, more collaboration, and more opportunity for social interaction. The third plane in many ways mirrors the first, as an egocentric phase that is given to tremendous brain growth. Junior students are looking towards adulthood, and their classroom gives them every opportunity to try on new adult roles.

Central to Maria Montessori's view of an educational system that is child centered and developmental by definition, the planes of development put a structure of common characteristics and tendencies around human growth from birth to 24 years of age. Thus, Montessori observed that children appeared to change into new individuals about every 6 years. She reasoned that if the child developed anew, then it followed that the learning environment and the adults' approach should also change. She stressed two points. First, if the child reached his or her full potential in the present plane, this created a firm foundation for the successive plane. Second, if the child did NOT realize his or her full development in one plane, he or she would still move into the next plane, but without the requisite academic and social skills. The first plane of development encompasses the years from birth to 6 years of age. Children from 6 to 12 years of age are in the second plane of development. Early adolescence to young adulthood (12 to 18 years old) is identified as the third plane of development. Finally, the 6 years between the ages of 18 and 24 constitute the fourth plane of development. In general terms, Montessori noted that the first and third planes are periods of tremendous transformation and construction, while the second and fourth planes are years of stabilization and strengthening. Each plane is also divided into two subplanes, each of 3 years in length.

Montessori schools are constructed and organized to support the kind of growth and learning that occurs within these developmental planes and subplanes. Toddler and Primary classrooms (first plane) share many like materials, lessons, and emphases, while still being distinct environments. The Elementary classrooms (second plane) represent a large change from the Primary years. While there are also significant differences between the subplanes of Lower and Upper Elementary classrooms, they are fewer and less salient. The Junior Class represents the first 2 years of the third plane of development and is another big jump. Knowing your child's developmental plane is an important step in understanding his or her needs and setting appropriate expectations.

The First Plane of Development—Birth to 6 Years. In Montessori pedagogy, the first 6 years of life are referred to as the first plane of development. These planes are further divided into "subplanes," each of which is 3 years long. We define these planes by the common physical, mental, and social characteristics shared by those within them. The first plane marks a time of tremendous physical growth (note the startling difference between a newborn and a 6-year-old!). Children in this plane tend to be on the chubby side, are more susceptible to illness, and are experiencing the growth of their first set of teeth. Mentally, children from birth to 6 years of age possess what Dr. Montessori referred to as an "absorbent mind." She makes a distinction between the first subplane (0 to 3 years), when children unconsciously and passively absorb their environment, creating movement, language, and the ability to control themselves, and the second subplane (3 to 6 years), when a personality is formed as the child perfects the faculties and powers absorbed earlier. The work of the hand becomes increasingly important, as does a sensitivity to order and the development of the senses. Parents and teachers alike will recognize this characteristic manifest in the child's proclivity for sorting objects by size, shape, color, sound, weight, temperature, etc. Iconic Montessori materials, such as the Pink Tower, the Broad Stair, the Red Rods, and the Knobbed Cylinders, are all examples of how a developmental need is met with the appropriate prepared environment. Further, children in this plane work to achieve independence and are internally driven to join a social group, including the family at home and friends at school. Socially, children from birth to 6 years of age are egocentric, viewing others as part of their environment rather than as separate entities. During the first plane of development, children are primarily interested in their immediate environment and the nomenclature and facts within it. Toddler and Primary classrooms are subsequently limiting, containing different materials and allowing for different activities which combine to support the child's growth. Materials for sensorial work, practical life skills, math, geometry, language, and the cultural subjects (biology, history, and geography) are explored with the senses, and long, uninterrupted work cycles provide the opportunity for children to repeat exercises to mastery. They are capable of controlling their movement and acquiring at least one language. Through the first 6 years, children in Montessori environments develop physical independence, knowledge, memory, will, and self-discipline.

The Second Plane of Development—Ages 6 to 12.
Maria Montessori identified children of 6 to 12 years of age
as being in the second plane of development. This plane is
marked by significant physical and mental growth. For
instance, children begin to develop stronger and more
complex reasoning. The first plane of development is
characterized as the "Age of What." The second plane is
referred to as the "Age of Why." A child of 4 years will ask
for the names of things: "What's that? What's this called?"
A child of 7 years is not satisfied with the label and instead
wants a deeper explanation:

Second-plane child: Why is it raining?
You: Because the clouds were full of moisture.
Second-plane child: Why?
You: Well... it has to do with the water cycle.
Second-plane child: What's a water cycle?
You: Do you want a cookie?

The child of the second plane is moving from a
concrete understanding to an abstract one. Consider the
materials for computation. In a Primary (3- to 6-year-olds)
classroom, children put together large addends by using
golden beads, ten-bars, hundred-squares, and thousand-
cubes. The sum is a real representation of the actual
quantity. In a Lower Elementary (6- to 9-year-olds)
classroom, however, quantity is represented using the
Stamp Game, a material comprised of square wooden tiles
of equal size, but "stamped" with quantities: units, tens,
hundreds, and thousands. Now numbers are given value by
using written numerals. The Bead Frame (an abacus-like
material) is a further "step towards abstraction," where a
bead gains its value through its position on the frame.
Mentally, the child in the second plane of development is

moving out of a sense of order and into a sense of the social world. Children begin to see others as coworkers and friends rather than just a part of the environment. The Elementary classroom environment is conducive to where the child is developmentally and supports the spontaneous formation of social groups. It is also a "dual" environment, encompassing both the child's classroom and the outside world, necessitating field trips to explore the greater society. And interests? For the elementary child, they include nothing short of everything. "Give the child the universe," was Dr. Montessori's exhortation to Montessorians. The curriculum, again moving from the concrete to the abstract in every curricular area, also moves from the whole to the specific. The cultural subjects start with the Big Bang and move from there into each scientific discipline. Human culture is a focus, as is the interrelated nature of the cosmos. Children leave the second plane of development with a level of self-confidence and intellectual independence. They have the ability to abstract and a love of learning as they move into adolescence.

Third Plane of Development—Ages 12 to 18. Maria Montessori identified children of 12 to 18 years of age as being in the third plane of development. Montessori noted that the first plane (birth to 6 years) and the third plane have much in common, such as significant physical and mental growth, a tendency towards egocentricity, and, of course, the desire for instant gratification. Both planes mark fundamental changes in being: birth into life and birth into adulthood.

In the third plane, the passage from concrete to abstract thinking is nearly complete. The Montessori environment responds to this development in several ways. Hands-on manipulative materials, which are so prevalent and essential in earlier classrooms, are no longer necessary.

They are replaced, however, by the tools and experiences of the adult world. Three-beam balances, gardening rakes, pH meters, hammers, and power drills continue the use of the hand as an instrument of learning, replacing puzzle maps, checkerboards, grammar symbols, and constructive triangles. Farm programs as well as a myriad of small businesses allow students to take on adult roles, work through the planning and execution of a project, and experience a feeling of accomplishment and positive feedback from both the school community and the professional world. That esteem carries over to the next project, and the cycle continues.

Another obvious difference is a more structured daily schedule, which allows the adolescent to take on the roles of "mathematician," "Shakespearean scholar," "harvester," "writer," "volunteer," "artist," etc., in turn. This predictable sequence supplants the long work cycles common to previous classrooms. Individual pacing within the academic subjects and independent work periods still provide elements of choice and freedom of movement.

Perhaps most significantly, the full development of an abstract mind is matched by the increasingly abstract subject matter. The ideas of the historical record versus myth, ethics versus progress, and the role of the individual in society serve as the tapestry upon which science, history, language, and humanities are stitched. Etymology, the nuances of meaning, and the difference between connotation and denotation serve as the backdrop to vocabulary acquisition and written expression. And the works of Shakespeare bring the full human experience to early adolescents, at a time when they themselves are also dealing with some of the same issues, e.g., insecurity, independence, jealousy, confusion, morality, and belonging, as Hamlet, Othello, Ariel, Richard III, Romeo, and Juliet.

Fourth Plane of Development—Ages 18 to 24. "The Child is father of the Man" is a William Wordsworth quote often attributed to Maria Montessori. It is clear why the phrase appears in many of her writings, as, in her context, it succinctly describes the fundamental rationale and purpose for the pedagogy that bears her name. Montessori's overarching theme was that fully actualized children are humanity's greatest hope for the evolution of civilization.

Maria Montessori identified adults from 18 to 24 years of age as being in the fourth plane of development. Dr. Montessori's enumeration of a finite number of planes might seem to indicate a completion, a culmination, an ending of sorts, even as it connotes a beginning, a rebirth into a fully adult stage. What constitutes that final plane of development? What tasks and what growth lay beyond the fourth plane? How does a Montessori education preface an adult life?

In pedagogical terms, we can identify a few characteristics of the age: metacognition, an awareness of one's potential, social maturity, and full independence. In the fourth plane, we develop a plan for ourselves, an interest in our life's work, a contribution to the greater society, and a sense of our own place in the larger global community. And the outcome of these 24 years, with four planes of development each fully realized in prepared Montessori environments, is a mature, independent, skilled, and responsible adult.

Spiritually, Montessori children evolve into Montessori adults. The concept of "cosmic education," which is the unifying knowledge of the universe that is so implicit to a Montessori curriculum, has been integrated into their lives. To their work, they bring a creative imagination, a confidence, a clear respect for their colleagues, and a remarkable self-awareness. In their politics, they advocate for peace and humanity, for personal accountability and responsibility, and for balance and fair play. In short, they realize that the living of a good life is in continuity with their childhood classrooms: productive and challenging, based on relationships with community, and filled with love and humor.

Thus, the planes of development inform our work, instruct the preparation of our classroom environments, guide our curriculum, and serve as the framework for the Montessori pedagogy.

Sensitive Periods

Maria Montessori used the phrase "sensitive periods" to describe the child's development within each plane. A sensitive period refers to a time when a child is especially in tune, especially ready, especially compelled to work on activities that satisfy the need of that developmental stage. It is temporary and, if missed, cannot be reacquired. A commonly understood example we can use to illustrate this concept is the acquisition of language. A child in the first plane of development is "wired" to acquire language in much the same way that a plant is "wired" to send out roots or begin to form a bloom. A child who is not provided an environment that supports this sensitive period for speech and communication will have a much more difficult task in attempting to acquire these skills at a later age. In the same way, Montessori identified 11 separate sensitive periods. When we speak of children being "inner directed," it is to these sensitive periods, a term borrowed from botany, to which we refer. Starting in the first plane of development, they include a sensitivity to movement, music, grace, courtesy, and order. During the second plane of development, from 6 to 12 years of age, the child develops a sensitive period for the use of imagination, for acquisition of culture, and for a strong sense of the social realm. There also exists a strong motivation for the learning of facts and nomenclature, as well as a sensitive period for the study of morality, right and wrong, and justice. A child in the third plane of development, from 12 to 18 years of age, is in a sensitive period for tremendous abstract thought, for delving into great detail on specific topics, for thinking in global terms, and for taking on adult roles.

The Prepared Environment

One of the key components of any Montessori classroom is what we refer to as the "prepared environment." In fact, Montessorians use the terms "classroom" and "prepared environment" interchangeably. At first glance, we might dismiss the term as being too obvious. Isn't every classroom a prepared environment in some sense? But as we discover more about the inner workings of the Montessori pedagogy, we find that the term is a rich and many-layered description. We can think of it as having three main components: the classroom materials, the adults (or "directresses" and "directors"), and the other children in the space. Physically, the classroom is arranged to be conducive to the children's independent, self-directed work. We notice low shelves, inviting materials, and work spaces both on the floor with work mats and at tables for both group and individual use. The hands-on materials are designed to meet the learning needs of the children in the relevant age group and are presented in lessons and then placed in the environment in a logical and sequenced manner. The adults in the classroom are well educated in the didactic use of the materials as well as in child development, and they actively support a classroom culture of challenging work, movement, and independent work. Lessons in responsibility, in grace and courtesy, and in sharing become part of the fabric of this environment, prepared to best suit a child's learning.

The prepared environment describes a classroom that has been laid out carefully and methodically to maximize the independent and spontaneous work of the child. The pedagogy is based on the foundation that children move through the different stages of development as part of their natural growth. They will independently acquire what they need if they are presented with the appropriate concepts, at an optimum age, with manipulative materials. Any effective environment for children needs to be set up in such a way that the children can access the materials, which are laid out in a logical manner, with a maximum amount of independence and a minimum amount of adult direction. Further, the classroom must be beautiful and peaceful in order to better allow each child's energies to flow without obstacles or distraction.

The Montessori materials themselves, as part of the prepared environment, also have a strong role to play. Besides their pedagogical function (hands-on, self-correcting, isolation of concept and difficulty), they too are objects of beauty. Montessori believed that working with quality materials, such as tongue-and-groove boxes, wood and glass pieces, and beads, is a crucial element to a child's learning that would be diminished if the materials were rendered in cheaper plastic, shabbily made, or easily broken.

Of course, we can also see that the term "prepared environment" must refer to more than the tables, the desks, the rugs, and the Montessori materials, to include the rest of the children in the classroom, the teachers, the daily schedule, etc. Thus, the role of the "teacher," which is better translated from Montessori's Italian as the "guide, directress, or facilitator," is less to talk *at* children than to prepare a classroom environment that will best facilitate a natural process already present in each child.

The Uninterrupted Work Cycle

In a Montessori classroom, we can broadly categorize the students' time in two ways. When the entire class is gathered, perhaps for the morning meeting or at the end of the day, the students are "on circle." This represents a relatively small fraction of their classroom time. The vast majority of a Montessori child's day is spent in a "work cycle." The work cycle itself can be divided further into lessons given by teachers and independent work time. Lessons from teachers during the work cycle can be presented on a one-to-one basis, in a small group, or even to the whole class. Independent work time represents the bulk of the work cycle, as students move through the classroom, selecting materials from the shelves and bringing them to a rug, desk, or table. Montessori environments strive to keep this precious time whole and undivided, attempting to keep interruptions to a minimum.

What does the work cycle look and sound like? A stroll around a Montessori school at any time from 8:45 a.m. to 11:30 a.m. or so, and again in the afternoon, reveals the essence of the uninterrupted work cycle. Children are working with friends on floor rugs and at small tables, or at single desks, manipulating learning materials, writing, illustrating maps, having a snack, and so forth. Teachers, who are not big voices and big personalities at the front of the classroom, are notoriously difficult to find, as they present lessons to students with subdued voices. They are also observing, redirecting, and sitting or kneeling at the children's level. A "Montessori buzz" is heard, that is, the volume is somewhere above library quiet but well below disruptive.

The uninterrupted work cycle is the heart and soul of a Montessori environment. Montessori spoke extensively about the need for children to develop their powers of concentration and focus in order to best internalize and integrate the concepts in which they were engaged. Learning research supports this idea. We learn best when we are focused on the task at hand. Thus, it stands to reason that a school should prioritize the creation of environments most conducive to developing the power of concentration. We cannot bemoan the lack of attention span in our children, blaming our undeniably "plugged-in," Internet-driven world, if in our schools we are equally at blame, interrupting students every 23 minutes to put away their math books and get out their language worksheets, or values clarification, or nutrition, etc. Instead, a Montessori environment allows children to develop longer periods of attention, and a sense of task completion, by protecting a work cycle measured in hours, not minutes.

The Montessori Materials

One of the strongest associations many people make with Maria Montessori is her development of hands-on learning materials. These are perhaps the most recognizable and prominent component of the "prepared environment," and they represent a powerful instrument of the pedagogy. The phrase "Montessori materials" refers to the beautiful hands-on manipulatives on the shelves of our classrooms. And while early educational theorists had developed didactic learning materials, it was Maria Montessori who realized and implemented their use with the greatest insight and success.

If you have heard your child talk about the Pink Tower, the Stamp Game, the Checkerboard, or the Trinomial Cube, these are all examples of Montessori materials. Likewise, puzzle maps, pin maps, grammar boxes, sentence analysis layouts, the Geometry Cabinet, and the Pegboard are Montessori materials. Specifically in Primary classrooms, your child is referring to the Metal Inset work (a material for the development and refinement of the hand), not what is sometimes misheard as the "Metal Insect" work!

Montessori materials have two main characteristics we can identify. First, the material represents an "isolation of difficulty." Simply put, the material does not attempt too much. For example, the Knobbed Cylinder material teaches discrimination of shape and size by using circumference and depth, but each set shows only one dimension. The second characteristic is the "control of error." An important aspect of the Montessori pedagogy is its support of independence in the child. By designing materials that are self-correcting, the work becomes more exploratory and more meaningful to the student. The use of bead chains, which are series of bead bars, each with the same number of beads, strung together, with corresponding arrows to label the multiples, illustrates this aspect. If a child mistakenly lays out a "48" label in the wrong position on the 8-chain, the error will eventually reveal itself, as only the multiples of 8 are present in the work.

The Three-Period Lesson

The term "three-period lesson" can refer to two aspects of Montessori pedagogy. Directly, it refers to the basic structure of a Montessori lesson, with each period corresponding to a section of the presentation. In short, the three periods are often illustrated as follows: "This is…" (first period), "Show me…" (second period), and "What is…?" (third period). A Lower Elementary teacher, for example, in giving a lesson on types of triangles, may present three different wooden triangles: a scalene, an isosceles, and an equilateral triangle. The first period of the lesson would consist of the giving of information and nomenclature. "This is a scalene triangle. All of its sides are of different lengths. This is an isosceles triangle. Two of its sides are the same, and one is different. This is an equilateral triangle; all of its sides are equal." The second period gives the child a reference point. "Show me the equilateral triangle. Show me the scalene triangle. Show me the triangle with three different sides. Show me the triangle whose name means 'same sides.'" The third period of the lesson removes that reference. "What is this? Which is this one?"

We can take the concept of the three-period lesson a bit further. We can identify experiences and activities that are giving information as the first period, activities that allow the children to work with the concept as the second period, and the presentation of work as the third period. In traditional classrooms, emphasis is placed on the first and third periods. "Here are the names and dates. In two weeks you will have a test and be asked to give back these names and dates." Seen in this expanded view, we can see that the vast majority of work in a Montessori classroom is much more meaningful second-period work, such as the activities of children working with the materials, finding similar concepts in the environment, making small booklets, creating timelines, or determining the areas of rugs in the classroom. The child ultimately arrives at "third-period" comprehension, but it is a more profound, internalized understanding.

The Great Lessons

Separate from the vast number of presentations given to children over their tenure from the Toddler to the Junior classroom, Montessori identified six Great Lessons, given in the second plane of development (between the ages of 6 and 12). In a sense, they are stories. At a time when a child's development is making full use of a burgeoning imagination, beyond the here and now and into the vastness of space and time, these lessons are meant to capture the child with an impressionistic presentation. They are an opening of a curtain to the drama of the universe.

The first Great Lesson is a Creation Story or its alternative, Life and Its Beginnings, which is the Montessori version of the Big Bang. This leads the child into discussions and work in geology, astronomy, and history. The second Great Lesson is the Story of Life, which uses the Timeline of Life as the chief material to present the evolution of life on Earth, from the early Paleozoic to the present day. This is followed by the Story of Humans, a lesson which employs two timelines, the first examining humans from the early australopithecines to *Homo sapiens sapiens* and the second inviting further study into just the last 25,000 years. The fourth Great Lesson is the Story of Communication, sometimes referred to as the History of Writing. A series of pictures and descriptions accompany this study, but it is also expected to be woven into the study of all subjects, including language, certainly, but into other curricular areas as well. Similarly, the fifth Great Lesson is the Story or History of Math. Much of this lesson is present in the myriad math and geometry presentations that explore the history of a particular concept at the same time that its presentation is given. These two lessons open up the study of ancient civilizations. And lastly, the sixth Great Lesson is The Great River, a metaphor for the human body system.

The Great Lessons integrate and spark an interest in all areas of our classrooms and are part of a larger framework that Montessori referred to as "cosmic education."

Cosmic Education

Cosmic education can generally be described as the unifying element in the Montessori pedagogy. Simply stated, it avers that all things are interdependent, that humans have a role in the universe, and that each of us have a "cosmic task." Cosmic education states, grandly, that a human developmental process underlies all growth and, further that education has a role to play in this development. It is the overarching theme of a Montessori classroom, a concept that is unique to the pedagogy, and the thread that holds the fabric of a Montessori experience together. It is a belief that theoretical structures, in all areas of study, should find practical use within our classrooms.

Cosmic education has four main aims. The first is to lead to the development of a whole human being. Academic achievement is not the only goal; rather, the goal is the realization of each child's natural potential. Learning involves the physical and emotional being, not just the intellect. The second aim is the formation of several types of relationships. These include the relationship between the child and the universe, a sense of marvel and respect for the vast scale of things, and an appreciation of the dignity of all things; the relationship between the child and the processes of life, creating a sense of the process of growth, an understanding of the role of cycles, and the perception of death as a continuation of natural law; and the relationship between the child and humanity, a realization of common needs, a celebration of diversity of culture, and the perception of oneself as a reflection of one's own culture. The third aim is the realization of responsibility, to all life, to the human species (through family, community, country, and society), and to self, through movement and reflection. Lastly, cosmic education endeavors to create a sense of independent action in the child, teaching him or her to take but give in return, to share willingly and with compassion, and to appreciate conscious and unconscious service.

And how is this implemented? A Montessori education leads children from the whole to the specific, displays the positive aspects of culture and history, employs concrete activities in the curriculum that lead to abstract concepts, uses impressionistic elements and emotions in lessons, and challenges students with ideas, while still providing reflective space towards the process.

Cosmic education, then, is not a singular area of study but rather a connective web that unifies the curriculum, providing both respect and responsibility to the child throughout the school years.

CHAPTER THREE
THE CURRICULUM

The Montessori method is an educational system that offers a rich curriculum including impressionistic lessons and manipulative materials offered in a prepared environment, with the whole process facilitated by trained teachers. Whew! Mention to a friend or relative that your child attends a Montessori school and you may get a variety of responses, ranging anywhere from a knowing nod to an arched eyebrow and an exclamation: "Really?!" While laying the definitions discussed above on the curious would be accurate, it may also result in a slow backing away, a glance at the phone, or an excusing of oneself in mumbles and vague references to other appointments. Thus, it may be better to learn a few basics of the Montessori classroom, the tenets if you will, that span age groupings and curricula, and go from there. The goal is to become better versed, and hence less intimidating.

Where to begin? An overarching theme is instructive as a starting point; in this case, the theme is a movement from the whole to the specific. In the study of geography, this manifests as presenting the entire globe to the child, before showing specific continents, followed by countries, cities, etc. In math, the first whole number represented is the thousand-cube, literally a thousand glass beads wired together. The cube in turn is composed of hundred-squares, each containing bars of 10 beads each. Single beads representing units completes the passage. In biology and history, an impressionistic, oral presentation of the Big Bang presages a study of the earliest life on earth, while the study of early humans is followed by a study of ancient civilizations. New information is built upon the foundation already laid. By giving the child the whole first, subsequent lessons and activities are integrated within a known construct. New information fits into previously learned knowledge, and a profound understanding solidifies.

A related and equally important theme is a movement from physical, tactile experiences to nonrepresentational and abstract concepts. In short, a Montessori curriculum moves from the concrete to the abstract. There exists a beautiful symmetry in this sequence of presentations and materials that mirrors a child's mental and emotional development. The Swiss developmental psychologist Jean Piaget exposited the concept of preoperational thought, which was marked by the child's inability to think symbolically. For a 3- to 6-year-old child, the physical representation of a concept actually is the concept, in a very real and concrete way. As the child matures into the elementary years, he or she is increasingly able to think representationally, metaphorically, and abstractly.

We see this framework of child developmental psychology paralleled in Montessori classrooms. (Note that this is not coincidental. Piaget was president of the Swiss Montessori Association, and Montessori was an advocate of Piaget's work.) A walk through a Primary classroom reveals shelves full of hands-on manipulative materials. In arithmetic, quantities are real. A unit is represented by a golden unit bead, and a 10 is represented by 10 unit beads on a wire. A 4-year-old adding 1,235 to 3,984 will do so with real amounts, i.e., actual beads. In geography, a 3-year-old cuts out a piece of clay to represent an island and pours a pitcher of water into the tray to surround it. In the elementary years and beyond, abstract and representational materials are presented to engage a child's mind that is now using imagination to grasp new concepts. A line and three circles—1,000—now represents the heavy thousand-cube of beads that a child held in his or her small hands just a few years past. There's an axiom in Montessori: "follow the child." Fittingly, this statement is true both in its concrete context and in the abstract.

We are describing, then, a pedagogy that integrates core curriculum areas with each other as well as with practical application. It uses the planes of development to correctly match a child's development to an appropriate environment, presentations, and manipulative materials. Montessori recognized that as children move through different ages, they have a window of opportunity to grow and learn in particular ways. She often used the analogy of a plant, with different "switches" being turned on and off as the seed germinates, sprouts into a seedling, and matures into a mature plant. Primary leaves grow at just the right time and then die off when no longer needed, while other growth takes their place. Likewise, a young child's receptors for language are engaged uniquely at birth to 3 years, in a way that cannot be repeated successfully when the child is older. In this way, the child moves in and out of the sensitive periods, for language development, for math, for culture, for moral development, etc. The 3-year age span in Montessori classrooms allows a community of children to move through these periods more organically and less tied to a specific year, in classrooms where they see their role change from youngest students to wise elders. And while

Montessori teachers are credentialed by the age level they teach (3- to 6-year-olds, 6- to 9-year-olds, etc.), there is an ample amount of crossover in material (i.e., the Stamp Game material for math is present in both Primary and Elementary classrooms) as children move into new spaces.

A Montessori education is distinguished in many ways, but perhaps to state it most simply, it presents the world from the concrete to the abstract (from hands-on activities to using paper and pencil) and begins this process early in a child's life. Lessons in practical life, the sensorial area, language, math, geometry, the cultural subjects (biology, history, and geography), and peace education serve as the framework for the curriculum.

Moving from the Concrete to the Abstract

An overarching theme of movement from the concrete to the abstract in a Montessori pedagogy can be discovered at each level. At the Primary level (3- to 6-year-olds), this can be seen reflected in the environment itself. Primary rooms contain three distinct areas: the sensorial, practical life, and academic areas, the latter of which is itself composed of arithmetic, geometry, language, and cultural areas. While these learning opportunities are available to all the children, they tend to have a particular developmental appeal and are selected by the students accordingly. For instance, a 3-year-old, who is likely a more concrete thinker, will be drawn more intently towards the sensorial materials. The Pink Tower, the Red Rods, the Broad Stair, and the Sound Cylinders are just a few of the many materials and activities that allow children to learn for themselves the distinctions between dimension and form, i.e., size and shape. Likewise, the practical life area, with its pouring works, polishing activities, and buttoning and zippering frames, also calls to a developmentally younger student. As the child matures, his or her attention is drawn to more challenging, more abstract, and more conceptual learning. In the Primary environment, this translates to the areas of language, arithmetic, geometry, and the cultural subjects (biology, geography, and history).

The advantages of a multiage classroom are manifold. An environment that encompasses learning materials ranging from the concrete to the abstract, and available to children over a 3-year age span, allows them to be successful where they are developmentally, regardless of their chronological age. This is not to say that a 5-year-old never uses the Lacing Frame, but one can speculate that for a 3-year-old it is a work of great concentration, while the 5-year-old uses it to take a mental break. And while the different areas of a Primary classroom are separated spatially, it is important that they are well integrated with each other. For example, the sensorial area serves as an indirect preparation for math, while the practical life area guides the child's fine motor skills towards the development of writing skills.

At the Lower Elementary level, this development can be understood most clearly if we discuss the scope and sequence of the arithmetic curriculum. The Lower Elementary arithmetic curriculum includes, among many other concepts, computation in whole numbers, using all four operations. As they enter the environment, children are, by and large, in the nascent stages of "formal" computation. By the end of this 3-year cycle, many, though certainly not all, will gain a facility with math facts and will be able to add, subtract, multiply, and divide abstractly, to some extent, using just pencil and paper and no materials. This example represents a remarkable academic, psychological, and spiritual journey taken within each student.

Through the use of manipulative materials, the child constructs an understanding of concept and a memorization of computation that eventually lead to abstraction. When we explore the materials and activities, it becomes obvious how they lead the child from stage to stage. Let's look only at addition and allow this specific study to serve as a microcosm of the whole. The Golden Bead material consists of individual golden beads, beads strung into ten-bars, bars wired into hundred-squares, and squares wired into thousand-cubes. Thus, a child adding two four-digit numbers is adding actual quantities of beads. As the child gains understanding, he or she will be presented the Stamp Game, which represents a large step towards abstraction. In this material, individual tiles are stamped with various place values (1, 10, 100, and 1,000) in the hierarchical colors for units, tens, and hundreds. The child, however, still lays out each quantity, making exchanges if a column's total exceeds nine. Next in the sequence of materials is the Bead Frame, an abacus that uses the same hierarchical colors as those in the Stamp Game and that represents another step towards abstraction. A bead on the Bead Frame gains its value by its placement on the wire, and there are only nine of each type; thus, this work is a triumph of representational thought!

In this way, in these years, the child develops the mental facility and imagination to see a digit as the quantity it represents. This growth continues as children move into the Upper Elementary environment. In Upper Elementary classrooms, we can see this evolve both in the use of the materials and in the curriculum itself. For instance, many of the math materials, e.g., the Checkerboard for multiplication and the Racks and Tubes for division, are designed to allow children to move from calculation using beads and bead bars to calculation done abstractly, using only pencil and paper. The repetition of process leads to memorization of algorithm. Other math materials allow the child to see difficult concepts, such as operations with fractions, percentages, geometry proofs, and the squaring of a binomial, as physical manifestations, making the abstract more understandable. That is, Montessori children can quite literally grasp the meaning of the math while wrapping their heads around the abstract concept being presented. And while math is a convenient and straightforward example of this process, it is by no means the only area of the curriculum that uses this structure. The study of grammar and sentence analysis at the Upper Elementary level, by its nature an abstract topic, is tethered to earlier concrete experiences, making the step away from the manipulative materials just that, a step. And a small one at that.

In a larger sense, the Upper Elementary child is also developing the ability to think more abstractly in terms of time. Whereas for a younger child each moment is either "now" or "not now," the older elementary child can think beyond the here and now to other lands and cultures existing across time. Further, Upper Elementary students can use this nascent imagination to see how their own lives perhaps would have unfolded across time and space. The curriculum responds in kind. History, geography, and science, known collectively as the cultural subjects (in the Montessori vernacular), have the study of ancient civilizations as a concentration. The 9- to 12-year-old child "takes these seeds of culture and germinates them under the heated flame of imagination." Leaving Upper Elementary marks the end of the second plane of development (6 to 12 years old). The child moves into the Junior Class, i.e., the third plane or early adolescence, and the concomitant development from concrete to abstract continues in new ways.

The entire pedagogy, encompassing children of 2 1/2 to 14 years of age, reflects the development in each child. A toddler enters a Montessori community, touching, stacking, and mouthing his or her way through the environment. Some dozen years later, the student graduates, but now postulating, considering, and coming to conclusions about the universe. Toddler to Junior: the former manipulates the physical, real, concrete environment, the latter the mental, psychic, abstract environment.

This transformative process also takes place within each plane of development. Smaller-scale evolutions from the concrete to the abstract in Toddler, Primary, and Elementary classrooms provide key manipulative materials at each juncture, matching the child's development with each step taken forward. The materials themselves do not teach. Rather, they provide a vehicle for children to make their own discoveries, create their own "a-ha" moments, and learn for themselves. The third plane of development, from 12 to 18 years of age (the first plane was birth to 6 years, and the second was 6 to 12 years), marks the start of adolescence. But even in these years of young adulthood we see the same change from concrete to abstract thought; it can be seen in several areas of the curriculum, but notably in the subjects of the humanities. The study of Shakespeare is often one of the stronger components of a Junior Class curriculum. As new readers to these classic plays, 13-year-olds are challenged by the vocabulary, often struggle with the meter, and take the histories, comedies, and tragedies at face value. The play is the plot, and the characters represent themselves. Under the guidance of a gifted teacher, these young adults begin to see the action as metaphorical, the plays as allegorical, the plots as representative of larger, more abstract concepts. Macbeth is more than a Scottish king, he is any power-hungry politician. Prospero is any puppet master adult. Iago is evil.

This harmony of purpose, providing the developmentally appropriate concrete materials to allow the child to internalize a great body of knowledge as the mode of thinking becomes more abstract, is a profound characteristic of a Montessori education.

Sensorial Materials

Perhaps the most recognizable materials in a Primary classroom are part of the sensorial area. The Pink Tower is one such material, and it is iconic enough to appear on the logos of many Montessori schools, as is the Broad Stair, the Red Rods, etc. A common observation of nearly all parents of 3- and 4-year-olds is the tendency to "order" objects. Give a child of this age a collection of stuffed animals, and more often than not he or she will line them up from tallest to smallest. A collection of cars will be classified by color. Shoes are neatly arrayed, and crumbs are removed meticulously from tables. I recall noticing my daughter at that age sweeping the loose dirt off of, well, a dirt path. The effort was there, though the result was somewhat frustrating as I recall. The Primary-age child possesses a developmental need, a strong need, to make these discriminations of form and dimension, and a Montessori Primary environment provides ample opportunity to satisfy it. Nearly any quality that CAN be ordered is represented. Along with the aforementioned Pink Tower and Broad Stair, the Color Tiles, Sound Cylinders, and Knobbed Cylinders all fill this developmental need. Touch boards with different surfaces, from rough to smooth, are present, as are baric tablets of different weights and cylinders with small button plungers that are increasing difficult to push down (they are ordered by pressure). There are even thermic cylinders into which the teacher places ice or lukewarm or hot water. The young child thrives in performing these differentiating and matching exercises, because they are precisely the activities children of this age need and desire. The developmental need for the sensorial materials is present at ages 3 to 6. The materials are not part of a Lower Elementary environment.

Practical Life

The term "practical life" refers to an integral part of the Montessori curriculum. While it is emphasized more at the Primary level, practical life is present in every classroom environment, from a Toddler to a Junior Class. Simply stated, the practical life curriculum refers to the materials, activities, and experiences that develop and refine skills for everyday living. As the child matures and moves into and out of sensitive periods, these activities change in nature but still remain.

In the Toddler environment, many, if not all, of the practical life exercises involve increasing the child's level of independence. Care of self, care of the environment, eating snack, getting out lunch, cleaning up spills, and getting dressed for outside play are all considered lessons of practical life. Montessori believed that the latter half of the first plane of development is a sensitive period for learning practical life skills, and we can see this clearly in Primary classrooms. A distinct area of the environment holds shelves that include a myriad of activities, such as pouring, tweezing, polishing, screwing, unlocking, buttoning, and zippering, that are all activities of practical life. Along with the sensorial and academic components, it completes the Primary curriculum. These activities have the added benefit of refining the child's fine motor skills, providing an indirect preparation for number and cursive writing.

Practical life skills in the elementary years include cooking, care of the environment, care of animals, and increasing contact with the adult outside world via field trips and other off-campus activities. In the Junior Class, practical life increases in prominence, taking the form of microeconomies and community service. Students operate small businesses, such as a farm, that allow them to have authentic experiences in bookkeeping and business as they sell products, not only to the school community but also, perhaps, to area restaurants. Opportunities for community service, such as being reading buddies, recycling, or volunteering, complete the program.

Language

Of the many distinguishing characteristics of a Montessori education, perhaps most important is the recognition that the years from birth to 6 years of age are times of tremendous mental growth and, further, that children in the first plane of development are in a sensitive period for learning, far earlier than traditionally thought.

The language curriculum in the Toddler House is the core focus for this group. The classroom is filled with songs, verbal games, rhymes, riddles, poetry, and conversation. Language also includes the use of extensive and correct vocabulary. At this stage, children are learning to communicate, and many say their first intentional word at 12 months. The Toddler House teachers encourage this development by constantly talking *to* the child, not *at* the child. The adults do not talk to students just to tell them what to do but also to tell them about the things around them and to describe what is happening. The environment uses books, singing, and rhymes to expand their vocabulary. Talking to them deliberately and clearly allows them to hear each sound and each word enunciated. To encourage language, the adults in the environment try not to overanticipate each child's needs. The Toddler House gives children ample reason to communicate, about food, about the learning materials, about sharing, etc. By not immediately responding to children as they point out objects or indicate something they want, the adults guide them toward developing a motivation for communication. Teachers name the item a child is requesting before giving it to him or her, so that later on the child will know what it is called and use the proper word for it. As children learn that there is a name for each object, they may start to point to things and wait for a reply from the adult as to what it is called. Favorite topics that children have at this stage of development are animals and the sounds they make, food, body parts, and transportation.

There is also no need for baby talk, so the adults name things properly and specifically. It is not just a "flower," it is a "red rose." The earlier a child is presented such vocabulary, the easier it will be for him or her to absorb such language, and this will be evident in later years. The "grace and courtesy" curriculum is also introduced at the Toddler level. Children are in a sensitive period for developing manners, such as saying "please" and "thank you" when appropriate. We can also observe that children's receptive language, i.e., language that they understand, is more developed than their expressive language, even as they become more independent and their movement abilities have increased.

While all major areas of the curriculum are introduced in the Primary classroom ("Give them the world!"), the acquisition of language takes precedence. The concept of "sensitive periods," times when certain areas of the brain are especially switched on to acquire certain types of knowledge, is easily seen here. We know that children cannot spend their first years bereft of language activity and simply catch up later. The window of opportunity for language opens and closes, and a Primary Montessori classroom takes full advantage of the absorbent mind of children of this age group with an environment rich in language. A Primary teacher recognizes that children are ready to express much more than they can physically write. Thus, the main impetus for learning to read and write comes from the child's own powerful desire to communicate and to decipher his or her own communication.

Language is, of course, omnipresent in the classroom. The nature of a Montessori environment requires the child to communicate with peers and teachers as a matter of course. In addition, manipulative Primary activities in language include the Moveable Alphabet, a box of individual letters that allow even a very young child to "write" without the fine motor control needed for writing with pencil and paper. Using Object Boxes, i.e., boxes containing miniature objects (a pot, a glass cat, a hat, etc.), and the Moveable Alphabet, Primary-age children form words by arranging wooden, and later paper, letters with their hands. Children are also presented lessons on letter formation with Sandpaper Letters, one letter at a time, tracing letters in both manuscript and cursive alphabets and later transferring the skill to paper. Often, a child in the last year of Primary education (an extended-day, or "'stended-day," child, in the local parlance) is presented with materials that bridge the Primary and Lower Elementary classrooms.

We can think of language in Lower and Upper Elementary Montessori classrooms in two different ways: first, as a distinct and separate area of the environment, and second, as a component that is integrated into the balance of the curriculum. The Primary classroom's language area is full of materials for the emergent reader and writer. Object Boxes, the Moveable Alphabet, Sandpaper Letters, and other materials, along with the lessons that present the relevant concepts to the young child, use both phonics and whole-language approaches. In the Lower and Upper Elementary classrooms (6 to 12 years old), while the materials still accommodate the nonreader, the emphasis on shelf work moves to parts of speech, word study, sentence analysis, punctuation, and advanced grammar. Many of these initial lessons are part of the extended-day child's afternoon in the Primary classroom, and these presentations carry over into the Lower Elementary classroom. Eventually, the material becomes increasingly advanced. Adverbs, first presented to 6- and 7-year-olds, are further subdivided into types of adverbs for 9- and 10-year-olds. Verbs, first learned in the Lower Elementary classroom, are further explored as transitive and intransitive forms in the Upper Elementary classroom.

The richness of the language curriculum in Montessori Elementary classrooms is largely evident, however, in its integration into the arithmetic, geometry, and cultural subjects. A child working on geometry is working with language. Learning the parts of the bird? Language is involved. Drawing a map of the gulfs of the world? Language is involved here, too. Reading and "command cards" in nearly every area support both reading and writing. A large share of writing, in fact, takes place in service of the cultural areas, with the child's writing lengthening in volume and complexity from the first year to the third. First, we see word-level writing on land forms. Next, we see short sentences describing the bodily functions of a reptile. Later, we see paragraph-level research on the history of shelter. It is the rare Elementary-level presentation indeed that does not involve reading, comprehension, and expression. Both initial presentations and the child's independent work later rely on the child's burgeoning abilities to code and decode language. Matching up cards to learn the parts of the fish? This is a vehicle for language. Studying a country? Yes, another vehicle for language. Learning the Pythagorean theorem, matching cards for timeline work, learning rules for adding fractions? All require language skills. Language is an integral part of every subject. And as the child moves into research, through the elementary years, it is done first at word level, then at sentence level, then paragraph level, and finally with paragraphs linked to form a short paper. The language area expands to poetry, spelling, writing for a specific audience, reading comprehension, fiction, nonfiction, etc. The elementary student's writing becomes more complex and is edited for style and content as well as mechanics. Language has become a tool that the Montessori student can use with confidence.

As Montessorians, we realize that children move into the Lower Elementary level with a wide variety of experiences and competencies in reading and writing; thus, they find a classroom that supports the nonreader and reader alike. The Moveable Alphabet, now on a smaller scale, with letters printed on paper and available in greater quantity, allows the emergent reader and writer to work with concepts of initial sounds, C-V-C word construction (consonant-vowel-consonant), etc. Daily instruction in reading and writing supplements the concrete materials, which include the Sandpaper Letters and other, "bridging" materials from the Primary classroom.

Other major components of the language area are word study, grammar, and sentence analysis. In Montessori, each part of speech is associated with a symbol (verbs are red circles, nouns are black triangles, adverbs are orange circles, adjectives are blue triangles, etc.), and these symbols are used to introduce grammar and, later, sentence analysis. The child's own written work becomes the subject of analysis and can now be used to identify parts of speech, using the appropriate grammar symbols described above. Eventually, the answer to the question "What is the action?" becomes the predicate, and the answer to the question "Who is it that...?" becomes the subject.

A child moving from the Lower Elementary to the Upper Elementary level (9 to 12 years old) is moving into the second half of the second plane. While this change is less of a developmental jump than the previous transition, it still represents a significant change. The language curriculum continues to move towards the abstract and towards greater specificity or detail. For example, the study of the parts of speech, introduced through a series of presentations referred to as the "Function of Words," identifies the nine parts of speech (verb, adverb, noun, adjective, pronoun, article, preposition, conjunction, and interjection). Working in more detail, the Upper Elementary curriculum explores the subcategories of the parts of speech (transitive and intransitive verbs, numerical adjectives, attributive adjectives, etc.), again moving from the general to the specific. Likewise, the actual wooden and paper shapes associated with the parts of speech are replaced by colored underlining. A verb is identified with a red rubber ball in the Primary classroom, with a red circle in the Lower Elementary classroom, and with red underlining in the Upper Elementary classroom. Sentence analysis also moves beyond the structure of subject-predicate-(in)direct object and into complex and compound sentences, with dependent and independent clauses and long adverbial and prepositional phrases. The Big Red Verb Box is an Upper Elementary material that delineates the differences in verb tenses, i.e., simple (present, past, and future), perfect, progressive, and perfect progressive, and verb voice.

A child's written work increases in volume and depth as well as style. Research papers are longer and are often accompanied by an oral presentation. A full range of writing styles—for persuasion, for description, expository writing, poetry, short stories, etc.—is presented. Word study and dictionary usage work continues, and more formal reading comprehension work and lessons in specific skills, such as finding the main idea or identifying inferences, are also part of the Upper Elementary (9 to 12 years old) language curriculum. By the end of the third year in Upper Elementary, students are moving into the third plane of development and are ready to move into the Junior Class.

Students come to a Montessori Junior Class with a solid foundation in language, including research writing, reading comprehension, and literature interpretation. The Junior language curriculum builds on this foundation and often integrates the subject area with a classical "humanities" approach, covering history, language arts, literature, cultural studies, geography, research projects, and writing. (And anything else that cannot be classified in traditional terms.) This curriculum uses a variety of texts, representative literature, and primary sources to discover the interconnectedness of knowledge.

The reading list in most Junior Class programs is rich and varied. As a basis for literature in the English language, it often features Shakespeare's plays, such as *Hamlet*, *Midsummer Night's Dream*, *The Tempest*, *Henry V*, *Macbeth*, and *Taming of the Shrew*. Other selections often include *Beowulf*,

To Kill a Mockingbird, Oliver Twist, and *Sherlock Holmes.* A Junior Class also makes extensive use of poetry, essays, and articles. Many Junior programs also make use of month-long and even year-long projects. These are in-depth research projects on a topic of great interest. The final project often includes an oral presentation, a visual and artistic representation, and a lengthy paper. Writing is also often supplemented by weekly "writing prompts," which are small freewriting experiences on myriad topics.

Geometry

Ask most adults about their experience with geometry when they were students, and you will get eerily similar responses. They hated it. And who can blame them? The geometry chapter in your math book was invariably the last one, the section you got to in June, squeezed between Memorial Day and Field Day. Both you and your teacher had thoughts of Summer Vacation (let's be honest, the statute of limitations had long since passed), obscuring any real learning. Strike One. Your textbook's approach to geometry, a study of shapes that is begging to be done with actual shapes? The textbook reduced it to two-dimensional diagrams on a page. The pedagogy? Use a series of "if/when" statements to prove a theorem. Want to make adult geometry-students-in-recovery flinch? Whisper the word "corollary" in their ears. Strike Two. And while young children are developmentally fascinated by shape and size and by exploring with their hands, we typically do not start the study of "formal" geometry until middle school. Strike Three.

During the first plane of development, the sensorial area serves as the vehicle for geometry. Observing a child stacking the Pink Tower, lining up the Red Rods, or using the Broad Stair, it is obvious to us that the child is exploring geometry. Geometric solids, i.e., cubes, spheres, ovoids, pyramids, and prisms, are traced (with fingers as well as on paper), their sides revealing other shapes and forms. The solids are nestled inside cloth bags, and children identify them by touch alone. Metal insets of triangles, squares, triangles, quatrefoils, rhombi, and parallelograms lead to further discovery of the nature of shapes. These heavy metal shapes inside frames can be placed atop cards printed with the corresponding outlines. The Constructive Triangles are also introduced at the Primary level, and this material will be used, in increasing complexity, through the Upper Elementary level. With this material, colored wooden triangles are used concretely to show that each quadrilateral (four-sided shape) can be formed (constructed) from two component triangles.

The geometry curriculum expands tremendously during the elementary years (note my restraint in not referring to it as a "geometric progression"), and a few new materials are introduced that will be workhorses for the next 6 years. The Box of Sticks is a material comprised of flat sticks of different lengths, with holes at each end in order to connect them to each other with clasps and/or to a cork board with tacks. With this material, the teacher can present and children can discover the constructions of any angle and any polygon. Complex tasks, such as finding the sum of the interior angles of a triangle (hint: it's 180 degrees), which would be done only theoretically in a traditional classroom, and even then probably not until high school, can be discovered joyfully by a 7-year-old who constructs a triangle from sticks, traces it on a piece of paper, colors and cuts out the angles, and physically puts them together. No matter what the shape of the triangle, the sum of the cut-out angles will always be a straight line. Amazing! Montessori would argue that this is a discovery of the first order. The "rule" may be well known to us and to the academic world, but for the child, it is personal. Think about that for a minute. Traditionally, we start with the rule and then prove it. In a Montessori classroom, we start with the experimentation and discover the rule. It is, and I won't restrain myself here, a 180-degree difference. As mentioned previously, the Constructive Triangles, used in the Primary (3 to 6 years old) classroom to show that quadrilaterals can be deconstructed into two triangles, are now used to show concepts of congruency, similarity, and equivalency. As the child moves through the geometry curriculum, identifying, classifying, constructing, and bisecting angles and discovering the relationships between them and to lines, he or she continues to use materials to support this learning. The Geometry Cabinet is a beautiful wooden piece containing six drawers with frames and insets of a myriad of shapes that can be used in an equal myriad of lessons and explorations. Later, metal insets allow the older child to discover the relationships between shapes and to answer questions. A triangle will be equivalent to a rectangle when what occurs? How do we arrive at a formula for the area of a polygon? And once we do, if we consider a circle to be a polygon with an infinite number of sides, can we use the same formula to find the area in squares of this shape defined by curved lines? (The answer is yes.) Even the Pythagorean theorem, an academic achievement so iconic that it is quoted when the Scarecrow gains his brain from the Wizard, is presented to the child in a series of metal inset "proofs."

Arithmetic

Maria Montessori recognized, before most educators of her time, the tremendous amount of development and potential for learning that existed in the first half (birth to 3 years) of the first plane of development (birth to 6 years). The age of the child was secondary to the primacy of the need to learn. She used the analogy that just as you cannot stop children from walking (they'll just get back up again!), the drive to develop and learn is natural, immutable, and unstoppable. A Montessori Toddler classroom, seen in this light, is a highly educational environment that invites exploration, practice, and skill building in all academic areas, just as surely as the classroom environment does for older students.

The purpose of the arithmetic activities in the Toddler House is to introduce number recognition, one-to-one correspondence, and simple counting (1 to 5, 1 to 10, and counting to even higher numbers when appropriate). Toddlers are curious about everything and need to touch and manipulate objects in order to learn. In the Toddler math area, simple concepts of numbers are introduced through songs, counting games, and manipulative materials. As the toddler works with manipulative activities, such as puzzles and counting objects, the toddler's understanding of number concepts and sequence gains substance. The use of knobbed puzzles and other toys with a special grip will prepare the child for writing and other fine muscle activities, while it satisfies his or her need to think and solve problems. The use of the thumb and index finger to form a pincer grasp, in particular, is a precursor for the motor skill required for writing. Many of the math activities in the Toddler House help the child to prepare for work and materials he or she will encounter in the Primary classroom.

Arithmetic at the Primary level, similar to geometry, has its roots in the sensorial materials, such as the iconic materials of the Pink Tower and the Knobbed Cylinders. The essence of this exploration of the senses is the distinction of form and dimension. While young children repeating these exercises are directly sorting blocks from largest to smallest, they are also involved in an indirect preparation for both arithmetic and geometry. The Primary math curriculum can be classified broadly into two subjects: numeration and computation. Numeration refers to the concept of quantity and symbol, namely, matching the quantity "four" with the written symbol "4." Whereas traditionally this work is postponed until the child is much older, and then shown abstractly with pictures on a worksheet, a Montessori classroom presents the concept to much younger children, when they are in a sensitive period to understand it, and uses concrete materials, allowing the child to actually roll four golden beads in her palm or feel the weight of a thousand beads fused into one large cube. Other materials that unite symbol and quantity are the Spindle Box, the Golden Bead material, the Number Cards, the Snake Game, and more. The second subject, computation, refers to the actual addition, multiplication, subtraction, and division of numbers. At this later point in development, there is a uniting of numeration and computation as children work out equations by using materials while reading and writing the problems out. Again, by using the Golden Bead material (unit beads, ten-bars, hundred-squares, and thousand-cubes, all golden hued), the Primary child has the concrete experience of actually exchanging 10 individual beads for a ten-bar and seeing the relationship of place value that is so crucial to the child's learning as she or he progresses through the curriculum. Many of the same materials in the Primary classroom are used again, with increased complexity, at the Lower Elementary level.

Children entering a Lower Elementary (6 to 9 years) environment are, developmentally, also moving into the second plane (again, Montessori defined human growth in four "planes," each of 6 years in length, starting with birth to 6 years, 6 to 12 years, etc.). Ideally, they have already spent the past 4 years in Toddler and Primary environments, and they arrive with rich experience gained through using the sensorial, arithmetic, and geometric materials. And while their new classrooms hold new teachers, new and older peers, and many new materials, there is also a wealth of available shelf work that is recognizable, but now used in a new way. One example of this evolution of material use is the short and long chains, the multicolored beads strung on wires in levels from 1 to 10 that we see displayed in both Primary and Lower Elementary classrooms. But while the younger child uses this work as a counting exercise, the 6-year-old is presented with the concept of "skip counting," placing arrows on the multiples of a given number. The short chains represent the square of a number, the long chains the cube. In this way, the very abstract task of learning one's multiplication tables is firmly rooted in the concrete.

Arithmetic materials are presented in sequence, moving the child from concrete representation to abstract reasoning and computation. The Golden Bead material that the 4-year-old uses to add and subtract with actual quantities is supplanted by the Stamp Game, where each tile (or "stamp") is the same dimension but now derives its value from the numbers (1, 10, 100, or 1,000) printed upon it. The Stamp Game, in turn, is replaced by the Bead Frame, where now a bead has value based on its position. The Stamp Game is used for all four math operations, the Bead Frame for all but division, the Checkerboard for multiplication only, and the Racks and Tubes for division. These materials are used for computation, while a variety of other materials, notably the Fingerboards, are used for the memorization of math facts. Other lessons are given for the concrete presentation of fractions.

Continuing within the second plane of development, children moving into the Upper Elementary classroom see continuity in the curriculum and materials from their Lower Elementary classroom. Many of the same materials are present here, such as the Checkerboard and the Racks and Tubes (for multiplication and division, respectively). The pedagogical movement here is the same as always in Montessori, from the whole to the specific, and from the concrete to the abstract. Specifically for math, the students move from computing using materials to computing using just pencil and paper. Children enter the Upper Elementary classroom with a wide variety of skill levels in arithmetic. In general, these children can add and subtract abstractly, can multiply using one-digit multipliers abstractly, and can divide with one-digit divisors. For more complex multiplication problems, children still rely on the Checkerboard, and for large division problems, they use the Racks and Tubes. Students leave the Lower Elementary level having been presented the concept of fractions as well as adding and subtracting fractions by using like denominators.

An important aspect of the Upper Elementary level is that while the curriculum becomes increasingly complex— indeed, much of the curriculum covered at this level is not covered until high school in a traditional setting—it still relies heavily on the use of materials. For instance, the Checkerboard was used for whole-number multiplication in Lower Elementary but transforms to the Decimal Checkerboard for decimal multiplication in Upper Elementary. Small "skittles" are part of Stamp Game division, serving as the divisor in a problem. Large skittles, which can be split into fractional sections, serve as the divisor in fraction division in Upper Elementary. The Pegboard, which is exclusive to the Upper Elementary environment, is used for squaring numbers and finding square roots. The large (and expensive!) cubing material is used, as its name suggests, for cubing and finding cube roots. Other subjects commonly covered include ratio and proportion, interest, and integers.

Children entering the Junior Class are also moving into the third plane of development, and into early adolescence. The changes occurring both physically, socially, and emotionally are as great as they have been since the children transitioned from the Primary to the Elementary classrooms. A Montessori environment responds to these new developments with changes in the classroom. Junior math programs generally consist of pre-algebra followed by basic algebra. Students work in math groups that meet daily to share problem-solving strategies, present projects, receive lessons, take quizzes, and support one another in the understanding of mathematics. Students also work at an individual pace on problem sets, puzzles, and tests, with a special emphasis placed on the process, i.e., showing all work to prove a solution. They formally correct scored assignments and tests in which they identify their errors as conceptual, arithmetic, or procedural. The study of economics, through the running of small businesses and microeconomies, includes a cost analysis of products which involves conversions, fractions, and operations with money. In addition, students effectively learn how to operate a checking account.

Cultural Subjects

The cultural curriculum in a Montessori classroom consists of three areas: history, geography, and science. As are all the component subjects of the Montessori curriculum, these subjects are integrated together, and with the pedagogy as a whole, including math, geometry, language, and the arts. Among the many contributions that Dr. Montessori bestowed upon the field of education, the approach to cultural subjects may be the most profound.

In her book *To Educate the Human Potential*, Montessori said that "knowledge can be best given where there is eagerness to learn, so this is the period when the seed of everything can be sown, the child's mind being like a fertile field, ready to receive what will germinate... all items of culture are received enthusiastically, and later these seeds will expand and grow." It is difficult to separate single threads from such a complex tapestry, as the cultural subjects are vehicles for so many other aspects of Montessori academics and the underlying message and themes that support them. The use of imagination, the concept of unconscious service, the Great Lessons, and Dr. Montessori's unifying vision, which she termed "cosmic education," are all excellent subjects, and have been excellent subjects, for previous and future essays. Therefore, for our purposes, we will take an overview of the triad of inquiry that makes up the cultural subjects.

History. Dr. Montessori was an optimist. She saw social ills and conflicts between nations as part of a larger process of "one step back, two steps forward," with the ultimate result of moving human civilization to a higher ideal. She metaphorically compared the study of history to a study of the railroads. If we were to teach children the lessons of the train system, would we only report the accidents and mishaps and show them merely the "broken carriages and twisted limbs"? Or would we instead instruct them on the miracle of exchange brought about via the railroad system, such as exchanges in trade and in humanity, revealing the grand lesson of human connection?

Similarly, she argued that looking at history as a series of wars is misguided. Instead, Montessori history focuses on achievement.

Geography. The study of geography is largely subdivided into three areas. These areas move from the concrete to the abstract, from physical geography to political geography to economic geography, as the child moves from younger to older classroom environments. Concomitantly, the curriculum moves from the general to the specific: from the creation of the universe to the study of the Earth, countries, states, and towns.

Science. A topic as expansive (and expanding) as the universe is presented to the child through a series of presentations and experiments, supported by impressionistic charts and biological timelines and in service to writing, reading, and research. Life is seen as a continual (and continuing) evolution of service, both conscious and unconscious, moving on, and in some cases off, Earth's stage.

The Montessori cultural curriculum is both simple and complex, representing two sides of a pedagogical coin. And while the content and structure of lessons and follow-up grow in step with the child, there exists a commonality throughout classroom environments, from the Primary level to the Junior Class.

Visit any Primary classroom, most any morning, and chances are you'll see a puzzle map out on the rug, with a child or two carefully taking each piece and tracing it on a large piece of paper. On the shelf there are two small wooden globes. The continents on one of them are all made of light brown sandpaper; the waters are smooth. Feel the rough land! On the other, the different continents are painted in different hues. Geography for these children is tactile. Later in the morning, a child celebrating their birthday walks around the classroom circle rug, with a glowing candle to represent the sun at its center (these days more likely to be battery operated). She cradles one of the globes as she makes her orbits, while her friends count each year. Hanging from the walls are large vertical timelines, with each year about a foot square. These are personal timelines, with a representative photo in each, along with a summary sentence or two ("My baby sister was born. We visited Grammy in Arizona."). In the afternoon, the entire class goes outside and collects leaves to bring inside. Wooden leaves from the leaf cabinet are taken out and their margins compared; they can then be classified into categories: pinnate, chordate, etc. There are other works to choose from as well. Which of these things float, and which do not? Which of these pictures show living things?

In Elementary classrooms, the tactile element is still a component of the cultural curriculum. To demonstrate basic land and water forms, the teacher cuts a piece of clay out of the center of a tray and places it in an empty tray alongside the first one. Water is poured into each tray, creating opposite forms: an island in one, and a lake in the other. Feel the land! Feel the water! Can more features be made? Yes! We can make gulfs and peninsulas, straits and isthmuses. Traced puzzle maps are labeled, and pin maps are introduced. Pin maps are wooden maps with small holes that hold pins to label countries, capitals, lakes, mountains, rivers, and seas. The Creation Story presages the science curriculum, which uses increasingly technical language. "These particles like each other" evolves into "They are saturate, they are super-saturate." The nature of elements, the sun and earth, the earth and its composition, the work of water, and the work of wind are areas of study that span the 6 years of the Elementary level. Demonstrated experiments are supported by impressionistic charts, which are repeated and expanded upon by the children. Another branch from the Creation Story trunk leads to biology. The Timeline of Life traces the movement of life from the oceans to land. Learning the parts of animals, fish, amphibians, reptiles, birds, and mammals is followed by learning the functions of animals: movement, protection, support, circulation, respiration, and reproduction. Botany follows a similar track, with experiments, charts, and card material allowing the child to work with parts, function, and classification. History is shown through a series of presentations, taking 6- to 12-year-old children from basic concepts of time through the history of civilization. The Upper Elementary years are traditionally given over to the study of ancient civilizations. The template of studying fundamental needs, both material (transportation, clothing, nutrition, and defense) and spiritual (spirituality, self-adornment, and art), serves as a guide for studying civilizations. Show us how a culture met its needs, and we will have a good picture of what that culture was like.

Most Junior programs take a humanities approach to the geography and history portions of the cultural subjects, using literature, primary sources, readings, lectures, written work, and oral presentations as part of the curriculum. "Humanities" is a catch-all term used to cover history, language arts, literature, culture studies, geography, research projects, and writing. (And anything else that cannot be classified in traditional terms.) Students use a variety of texts, representative literature, and primary sources to discover the interconnectedness of knowledge. Science is often presented in "blocks" of 6 weeks or so, covering physics, botany, zoology, earth science, and astronomy, with a greater refinement in nomenclature and procedure, write-ups and reports, and using the scientific method.

There is great variety in Junior or Middle School models in Montessori schools worldwide, a result of less specific articulation by Dr. Montessori herself. An appendix to one of her books is one of the few expositions she or Mario (Maria Montessori's son) made on the subject, leaving most schools to conjecture on how to implement a Montessori program for this age group.

CHAPTER FOUR
THE CLASSROOM ENVIRONMENTS

Toddler

At what age does a child become a student? When I describe Montessori schools in terms of the school population, there is a moment of hesitation when I note that there are "students" as young as 18 months old. Really? Aren't they still just children a few months north of babyhood? Dr. Montessori said, "The senses, being explorers of the world, open the way to knowledge." A Montessori Toddler environment demonstrates with clarity the move from concrete to abstract thought that every child develops. (Note that "abstract" in this context refers to the use of language. The physical reality of a ball is symbolized by the toddler with the sounds "buh-all."). At this age, the child is learning everything through his or her senses, and the environment is especially prepared with this in mind. Manipulative materials allow the child to explore concepts of shape, space, number, sound, touch, and color; the possibilities are myriad. These sensorimotor activities allow the young learner to generalize concepts through hands-on and, in some cases, "mouths-on" experiences. In a very real sense, the child is undergoing the process of perfecting him- or herself, which is pretty heady stuff for a 2-year-old!

At the same time, a burgeoning sense of independence develops, and toddlers begin to acquire a keen interest in the care of both themselves and their environment. Again, a Montessori Toddler classroom meets this developmental need by offering materials and activities specifically suited for a young child's sensibility and size. Washing and drying dishes, zipping and buttoning clothes, opening and closing containers, and sweeping and dusting floors and furniture (try this at home!) allow the child to interact with the environment while perfecting his or her body movement. In a Toddler classroom, therefore, as in all Montessori environments, learning takes place through a child's experience, not through what a teacher "does." While there are schools that offer an Infant/Toddler program, complete with cribs and rocking chairs, most schools that maintain a pre-Primary program serve the needs of children starting from 18 months of age. In Montessori pedagogy, children at this age, between birth and 6 years, are in the first plane of development. A further subdivision, halfway through the plane, separates the Toddler program (birth to 3 years) from the Primary classroom (3 to 6 years). The environment conforms to the physical needs of the children, both in the size of the furnishings and in the opportunities for motor development. There is an observation area for adults, minimal furniture, warm hardwood floors, maximum natural light, selected art placed low on the walls, toilets sized for very small children, and defined spaces to challenge coordination of movement. The environment has three distinct areas. The movement area includes stairs and a platform; a movement mat; materials for practicing eye-hand coordination, such as threading, bead stringing, stacking cubes on pegs, placing spheres on horizontal pegs, putting puzzles together, gluing, and folding; and various practical life exercises. The practical life area includes materials necessary for preparing and serving a snack, setting and clearing the table, sweeping, caring for plants and animals, washing dishes, washing clothes, ironing, polishing, washing hands, cleaning windows, arranging flowers, and so on. The language area includes miniature objects, language nomenclature cards (parts of the body, family members, pets, and components of the neighborhood, the school, and the home), books (fiction, poetry, and nonfiction), spoken vocabulary enrichment exercises, and other activities, including art and music experiences. Children with a foundation in the Toddler House move into their Primary classrooms already experienced in social interaction, prepared for independence, and cognizant of the classroom as a resource for their own development.

Primary

Primary classrooms are environments that serve children between the ages of 3 and 6 years. The classroom environment has three components, each of which supports and reinforces the other two: sensorial work, practical life, and academics. The sensorial area contains all the activities for discrimination of dimension and form, i.e., size and shape. The materials include the Pink Tower, the Red Rods, the Broad Stair, and a host of other manipulatives. The practical life area contains pouring works, buttoning and zippering frames, polishing activities, simple bolt-and-screw trays, and washing tables. These materials feed children's increasing need for independence and a tendency to want to repeat the activities they see older siblings and parents performing. The sense of order dominates here, as seen clearly in the first two areas but, in a larger sense, in the rest of the environment as well. We can use the term "academics" to identify the balance of the environment, which consists of shelves that contain materials for learning arithmetic, geometry, language, and the cultural subjects. It is important, however, not to lose sight of the integration of all three areas. Certainly a child stacking the Pink Tower is discovering relationships in geometry, and the child carefully moving cotton balls from one container into another will use this skill when it comes time to pick up a pencil. Nomenclature is emphasized as well, throughout the environment. In fact, this age is often referred to as the age of "What?"

Elementary

In Montessori pedagogy, children at the Elementary level, or between 6 and 12 years of age, are in the second plane of development. For practical reasons involving physical space, a further subdivision, halfway through the plane, separates the Lower Elementary classrooms (6- to 9-year-olds) from the Upper Elementary classrooms (9- to 12-year-olds), but it is important that we consider the Elementary program to be one united curriculum, one united environment. While there are differences between the Primary and Elementary environments, of course, they are differences in the materials found on the shelves and are countered by more similarities. Children continue to choose their work from among the self-correcting materials displayed on open shelves, and they work in specific work areas, but the areas themselves have changed. The sensitive period for sensorial works has closed and is not part of the Elementary environment. Likewise, the practical life area in the elementary years takes the form of cooking, caring for the environment, and taking field trips and is no longer a "shelf work."

If the Primary level is the age of "What?," then the elementary years are the age of "Why?" Exploration of shape and form gives way to an interest in nomenclature and a discovery of the relationship between things. Montessori described the mission of the Elementary curriculum as "sowing the seeds of culture, to germinate under the flame of excited imagination" (she spoke that way sometimes). When asked how much of the world's knowledge should be shared with elementary children, she responded, "All of it."

The Elementary program offers a continuum built on the preschool experience. The environment reflects a new stage of development and offers an integration of the arts, sciences, geography, history, and language that sparks the imagination and abstract mind of the elementary child. Presentations of the formal scientific language of zoology, botany, anthropology, geography, geology, etc., expose the child to accurate, organized information and respect the child's intelligence and interests. The use of timelines, pictures, charts, and other visual aids provides a linguistic and visual overview of the first principles of each discipline. In this manner, the child gains knowledge, certainly, but as part of a large-scale narrative that unfolds the origins of the earth, life, human communities, and modern history, always in the context of the wholeness of life. As in the preschool, the Montessori materials are a means to an end. They are intended to evoke the imagination, to aid in abstraction, and to generate a world view about the human task and purpose.

The Romance of the Elementary Years. Alfred North Whitehead was an English mathematician and philosopher who also wrote frequently and eloquently about education. He was a contemporary of Maria Montessori (though I have yet to find any record of them actually meeting), and it is instructive to examine how their thoughts on pedagogy overlap.

Whitehead saw the learning process as having three components, which he labeled romance, precision, and generalization. In the romance stage, the child is first presented with a new concept and enjoys the emotion of discovery. According to Whitehead, the child is "becoming used to curious thoughts, of shaping questions, of seeking for answers, of devising new experiences, and of noticing what happens as the result of new ventures." Picture a child's first experience at a beach strewn with shells of various shapes, sizes, textures, and colors. The child is given to the visceral excitement of the moment as he or she explores the myriad stimuli present. If this energy is acknowledged and supported, Whitehead asserts that a second desire will arise, one that craves deeper, more precise information to answer the very questions that the stage of romance engendered. The child, home from the beach, pulls out shell identification books and the "S" encyclopedia and excitedly learns the types, biology, and nomenclature of shellfish. Whitehead made a point of noting that traditional education puts an emphasis on just this second stage of precision: the facts, the specifics, the right and wrong. But without the more general, broader view that comes from the romance stage, he argued, the facts are barren and nebulous, unattached to any larger context, and quickly forgotten. The third stage of the learning process is that of generalization and synthesis. It is a stage that leads the child further, allowing the integration of this newfound information into creative ideation and a cogent "whole." It also, quite elegantly, leads the child back to the first stage of romance, of discovery, but with the addition of this gained wealth of knowledge. Subsequent excursions to the beach equal the excited discovery of the first trip, but the experience is now imbued with a greater sense of wisdom, as the specific is now seamlessly integrated with the whole.

A basic primer in Montessori would doubtless include a definition of the three-period lesson. Taking the task literally, it would illustrate the basic parts of a Montessori lesson, as follows. The first period is the naming of the new information. For instance, a geometry lesson on types of triangles would commence with their identification, using wooden sticks for their construction. "This is a scalene triangle, this is an isosceles triangle, this is an equilateral triangle." The first period is often impressionistic and dramatic (though, admittedly, as a teacher you'd have your work cut out for you in this particular example). The second period involves the referencing of the information given in the first period. "Show me the isosceles triangle, show me the scalene triangle." Similarly, questions such as "Show me the triangle with three equal sides" are considered second-period questions as well. The third period eliminates the reference and serves as a confirmation of the learning. "What is this triangle? And this? How about this triangle?" In Montessori slang, if you will, the three-period lesson is sometimes referred to as "This is…, show me…, and what is…?"

Thus, on a superficial level, the three-period lesson is a structure upon which a holistic lesson is built. However, we can expand our definition of the first period to include the reception of any new information by the child. We can expand the definition of the second period to include any activity in which the child works independently with the material. And we can think of the third period as any demonstration of mastery or apparent felicity with a concept by the child.

Whitehead argued that a failing of traditional education lay in the de-emphasis of the romance stage, the laying down of the contextual foundation. Similarly, Montessorians would argue that a traditional pedagogy deals almost exclusively with the first and third periods. Students are given information and then told that they will be quizzed on particular dates in a week's time ("Here are some historical dates to memorize; I will test you on them."). The emphasis in a Montessori classroom is on the second period, the child's work. The teacher-involved first and third periods pale in comparison.

Junior Programs

In the wealth of Montessori literature, there is relatively little written about the 12- to 18-year-old age group. The vast majority of Montessori's work dealt with children between the ages of 3 and 12 years, and we are left with an appendix in the book *From Childhood to Adolescence*. In her more general work, Montessori referred to these years as the third plane of development. The Junior Classes, regardless of how they are named, provide an environment for the first half of the third plane, a 12- to 14-year-old grouping that would translate to the 7th and 8th grades in a traditional school. It is important that the move from the Upper Elementary environment to the Junior Class represents a change from one plane to another, and is therefore more significant than the transition from the Lower to the Upper Elementary group. Seen this way, it is more apt to compare this move to the transition of children moving from a Primary classroom to an Elementary classroom.

What Montessori did outline for these early adolescent years she referred to as "Erdkinder," or "Earth Children." She envisioned young people leaving their families and their traditional schoolrooms and boarding at an inn and farm that they would manage. The running of this business would provide hands-on mathematics work, the farm would provide a curriculum in botany, and likewise breeding livestock would provide a curriculum in zoology. Removing children from the social crucible of life in a large junior or middle school and giving them access to the land were the main impetuses behind such a concept, but there was also a recognition of the need for early adolescents to participate in authentic, "real" work, trying on adult roles in a safe place and on a small scale.

Many Montessori schools modify the Erdkinder concept by integrating work in microeconomies, with a comprehensive curriculum in language, math, geometry, history, and science, as well as opportunities for students to work a farm and to harvest crops for sale. Basil becomes pesto, and sage and thyme are sold both fresh and dried. A study of acids and bases in science lends itself to a service providing pH testing for garden soils. The building of a stone garden wall dovetails with a study of Frost's "The Mending Wall" in language. The need to "get out" into the world continues. This takes the form of weekly community service at soup kitchens or academic study trips.

CHAPTER FIVE
UNDERLYING LESSONS

Montessori schools have long relied on the successes of their graduates and on word of mouth to validate their programs. Results are self-evident in the happiness, well-being, and learning success of the children. In the last decade, however, an increasing amount of empirical data supports what Montessorians have long known, that this pedagogy is unsurpassed as a model of education for a wide variety of students and learning styles. The pace of research has been geometric in its growth. In fact, there have been more studies related to Montessori done in the last 2 years than in the previous 10 combined. In *The Science Behind the Genius*, a landmark book released in 2005, Angeline Lilliard outlines current scientific research that provides astounding support for the Montessori method. Lilliard presents the research concerning eight insights that are foundational to a Montessori education and describes how each of these insights is applied in the Montessori classroom. It provides a clear understanding of what happens in a Montessori classroom and, more importantly, why it happens and why it works.

A myriad of studies have also appeared in periodicals and journals. The September 2006 issue of *Science* detailed a study comparing outcomes for children at a public inner-city Montessori school with those for children who attended traditional schools indicating that Montessori education leads to children with better social and academic skills. A study sponsored by the Association Montessori Internationale (AMI) supports the hypothesis that a Montessori education has a positive long-term impact. "A significant finding in this study is the association between a Montessori education and superior performance on the Math and Science scales of the ACT and WKCE. In essence, attending a Montessori program from the approximate ages of three to eleven predicts significantly higher mathematics and science standardized test scores in high school." Another interesting study involves the concept of the "flow experience." A flow experience is analogous to being "in the zone," or in a state of high concentration or focus, where there exists an especially great potential for learning to take place. *A Comparison of Montessori and Traditional Middle Schools: Motivation, Quality of Experience, and Social Context,* by Kevin Rathunde, compared the experiences and perceptions of middle school students in Montessori and traditional schools. Montessori students reported a significantly higher quality of experience in their academic work than did traditional students. In addition, Montessori students perceived their schools as a more positive community for learning, with more opportunities for active rather than passive learning. It is gratifying to see such research being done, and confirming what we knew all along. A pedagogy that has been successful for over 100 years must be doing many things right.

Learning and Memory

Memory and learning are positively affected by many factors. These include choice, classroom structure, spatial organization, context, interest, imitation, familiarity, mastery challenge, movement, narrative, and repetition. Looking at each of these in turn reveals examples of ways that Montessori environments support each one.

Choice refers to the learner having an element of decision-making in the task. Simply stated, when we can choose our tasks, we learn better. That independence is an integral part of the structure of a Montessori environment. Spatial organization, where what we are learning is laid out in organized fashion, is both a great aid to memory and a description of a Montessori prepared environment. When what we are learning is in context, we are much more able to absorb the material. In a Montessori curriculum, cosmic education is the unifying concept that places everything in context, showing the interdependence of all subject areas. Another example from our classrooms involves interest. In math, for instance, the Primary curriculum uses large numbers and large concepts to captivate the young child's imagination. Where there is interest, there is learning. A strength of a multiage classroom is that it allows imitation. Seeing another child work on a task or with a material is a great aid to the observer's learning. Similarly, when things are familiar to us, it is much easier for us to assimilate information. The hierarchical colors used as a mnemonic device in math (green shows units, blue shows tens, and red shows hundreds) are an example of using familiarity to instruct. Montessori classrooms are replete with independent challenges. With its diverse materials, from the Long Chain of Nine to the layout for the Timeline of Life to the pin map of the capitals, the environment offers children many opportunities for mastery challenge, yet another aspect that greatly increases learning and memory. Movement, both gross motor and fine motor, also appears to support an understanding of material and is, of course, a large part of both the Montessori classroom and its manipulative materials. Many of the lessons in the curriculum call for storytelling, using the context of a narrative to support memory. And a final aspect of learning is repetition. We learn better, and more efficiently, when we can repeat an exercise, a concept that is foundational in Montessori.

Choice. "But how does a child know what work to choose to do?," is a common question on tours. We stand in the hallway outside any classroom, observing children who are, for the most part, energetically engaged with the environment. They move purposefully, taking work off shelves and finding places to work. This is a fair question. It also speaks to a common misconception about Montessori, sometimes expressed as, "Montessori just lets children do whatever they like." Well, yes. And no.

A well-prepared Montessori environment responds to a number of needs, allowing a child to do the important work of self-development. Some growth can be observed overtly: a child learns to count, to write a sentence, or to find the square root of a radicand. Other developments are less apparent: a child gains understanding, budgets his or her time, or feels empathy. But, arguably, the most important factor involved in this development is the element of independent choice. A Montessori education expressly provides for this "inner growth," just as surely as it provides an academic foundation. Starting as early as the Toddler program, a Montessori environment develops a sense of appropriate activity: how to use a material, how to take it from and replace it on a shelf, how to share, and how to choose works from a variety of areas. A child in this type of environment develops an inner discipline that informs his or her choices regarding both behavior and work. Coercion from an extrinsic force, such as an authoritarian teacher or someone else's expectations, can achieve a similar appearance, but the liberty that comes from self-control developed from within is so much more profound. That sense of knowing what to choose is, of course, supported by peers, by teachers, and by structure, in the form of guidance and planning and negotiating. Ignoring math for an extended period is not an option, but the choice of when and where is always present. Studies show that even the expectation of choice, regardless of whether it is exercised, improves student learning (see Chapter 3 of A. Lilliard's book *The Science Behind the Genius*). It is no surprise that an environment and pedagogy that stress independent choice allow such well-grounded children to develop and thrive.

Spatial Organization. An important component of a Montessori pedagogy is the "prepared environment." This is a Montessori term that refers to the physical classroom, but even beyond the learning materials it contains, the prepared environment facilitates learning in its organization alone: the placement of materials in sequence, the layout of shelves, the simplicity of design.

Montessori classrooms are called prepared environments to emphasize the care that goes into their layout. An intentional spatial organization exists in every Montessori classroom. While perhaps no two classrooms look exactly the same, a continuity exists that binds each together. In a Toddler classroom, there are areas for both gross and fine motor play, an area for books, and an area for lunch preparation. In Primary classrooms, there are sensorial and practical life areas as well as areas for arithmetic, geometry, language (emerging reading and writing), and the cultural subjects (science, history, and geography). During the Elementary years (6 to 12 years), a Montessori student finds a classroom that no longer has a sensorial or practical life area and instead has more fully developed areas to contain materials for arithmetic, geometry, cultural subjects, and language. For example, the language shelves now contain new content, such as materials for learning grammatical nomenclature, sentence analysis, reading comprehension, etc.

Spatial organization leads to greater and deeper learning. Studies conducted outside the realm of Montessori, and independent of it, bear this out. For instance, in one study, two groups were given a list of minerals, one as a random collection of names and the other in an organizational "tree." The group that studied the list in a hierarchical form was much more likely to both remember and understand the material. Other studies have found a correlation between academic performance and the level of organization of the child's home space and schedule (this is, perhaps, a terrifying revelation for some). The prepared environment does more than just contain Montessori materials. It creates a mental framework for children as they choose their work and experience the depth of this integrated curriculum.

The Role of Interest. Most adults observing a Montessori classroom are quick to notice its strengths. The use of manipulative materials, the small group lessons, the beauty of the prepared environment, and the freedom of movement all form an impressive tableau. A more in-depth observation would also clearly reveal the integration of subject areas, the social interaction, and the element of choice. Within that structure, students move with purpose (most of the time) and ease, seemingly without adult compulsion. Children voluntarily seek out activity, come to lessons willingly and happily, work with peers of their own accord, and, with guidance, take responsibility for their education. The structure for this drive does not come from a draconian adult or some other extrinsic force. Instead, the children appear to have an intrinsic urgency to act upon the environment. Why?

A crucial aspect of any Montessori classroom is perhaps less discernible due to its conspicuousness. The driving force in the child's interaction and progression through the curriculum is deep interest. It is the tree that cannot be seen for the Montessori forest. This passion is created through creative and impressionistic lessons, the presentation of grand concepts, the use of large numbers, the emphasis on the power of imagination, and the liberty to choose a compelling activity for oneself. Beyond providing a natural incentive, interest further serves as a powerful tool for learning. Studies clearly show that we are much more likely to assimilate information if it holds strong interest. One such study had participants list a series of articles in terms of their interest. Not surprisingly, comprehension scores on these readings mirrored the rankings the individuals had given. Areas of higher interest naturally hold our attention, heighten our focus, and compel us to iteration and practice. Consequently, the learning that takes place is more meaningful, more profoundly held, more deeply understood, and more logically connected and synthesized. And need we mention joy? Thus, at the end of the day (the metaphorical day, not 3 o'clock dismissal), it is the child's likely response that speaks volumes in its simplicity. "Why do you like going to school?" "It's fun."

Learning in Context. Research supports what we all realize intuitively: we learn best when the content of the lesson is provided in context. A simple study, but one of many, comparing the memorization of a set of medical terms, one given to student nurses and one given to a control group, showed that when we are given information in context, in this case for those entering the medical field, we are much more likely to absorb the concept.

A Montessori education provides a rich and integrated curriculum that stresses learning in context. The study of geometry includes a study of its Latin roots, a study of unlike denominators in arithmetic includes the writing of the rule "change the denominators first", a study of an ancient civilization coincides with a study of rivers, and pH studies evolve into soil testing. Specific Montessori materials can also reflect this sense of context. For example, the Detective Triangle Game, located on the language shelf, consists of a box of triangles of different types (scalene, isosceles, etc.) in different colors and of different sizes. Labels accompany the work, giving instructions such as "Find the large, red, equilateral triangle," thus presenting geometry as a grammar work. Speaking more broadly, the concept of Cosmic Education, which is unique to this pedagogy, is the overarching theme of a Montessori classroom. It holds the fabric of a Montessori experience together and places everything the child learns in context.

The Role of Imitation. Everyone knows that imitation is the sincerest form of flattery, right? While this may or may not be true, it is certain that imitation is also a powerful learning tool. Studies abound illustrating the human tendency to mimic, both consciously and subconsciously. Participants watching a video featuring rude exchanges between actors are liable to be rude themselves when put in social situations immediately afterwards. It is clear that as a species, we are profoundly influenced by the people that surround us, and this can impact both our actions and our learning.

How does this manifest itself in a Montessori environment? One clear component is the multiage classroom itself, an aspect that holds many advantages for students, parents, and teachers. Children enjoy the security and comfort of staying in one room for 3 years. Parents do not have to reintroduce their child's strengths and challenges to new teachers each September, and they know that the teachers will gain a deeper understanding of the child's needs during the 3-year cycle. For teachers, the variety of ages and developmental stages in the same classroom allows them to move more freely through a scope and sequence of study, as the so-called "shotgun" approach, requisite to a single-age classroom, is not necessary.

As important as these elements are, Montessorians have known all along that there are also clear pedagogical advantages to a multiage classroom and the opportunities it affords to use imitation as a tool for learning. Younger students watch older students, hear the language of the lesson given on the next rug over, observe the use of more complex learning materials, and mirror their behavior. This is why we often hear Montessori teachers emphasize to these older students their role as models and peer teachers. And, of course, the teachers themselves give lessons in such a way, with great care and exaggerated movements, as to stress key elements in any given lesson, for example, the 30 steps to washing your hands. We can see how Montessori's use of the phrase "the absorbent mind" reflects her understanding of the importance of imitation.

The Role of Familiarity. Many Montessori schools have the great benefit of a full complement of Montessori programs. Toddler students, beginning as early as 18 months of age, will stay for as many as 13 years before they graduate from a Junior Class as eighth graders. Their familiarity with the building and grounds, the people, and certainly the pedagogy is a great comfort to both children and their parents. But familiarity also has great benefits in an educational sense.

Piaget, himself the president of the Swedish Montessori Society, performed a well-known test called the "mountains study." He put children in front of a simple plaster mountain range and then asked them to pick from four pictures the view that he, Piaget, would see from where he was sitting. The test was initially used to show a child's development in visual-spatial awareness, namely, that children younger than age 7 were egocentric and unable to see another's viewpoint. However, a follow-up study using a scene familiar to children, i.e., the setting and characters from Sesame Street, rather than the completely foreign Swiss Alps, showed that the familiarity of the setting had a dramatic effect on the children's learning.

A Montessori environment makes use of this principle in myriad ways. The most visible example of this concept is the "hierarchical colors." When children near the age of 5 years, the Stamp Game is used to introduce a mnemonic color-coding scheme for place value. Units are green. Tens are blue. Hundreds are red. Thousands? They are green, because thousands are still units, just units of thousands. These hierarchical colors are then used as a constant device as the child moves towards more complex and abstract math. The Bead Frame (for addition, subtraction, and multiplication), the Checkerboard (for multiplication), and the Racks and Tubes (for division) all use the same identifying colors. The colors of the short and long bead chains, the colors that correspond to each part of speech, all serve as a conceptual grounding for the child, a link to the concrete experiences that preceded it, and a guide to further exploration. The material is new and the concept is more complex, but the familiarity of color (or shape, or timeline, etc.) isolates the difficulty and frees the mind.

Kindness

One positive aspect of the social media explosion is the ease of staying in touch that it affords. Alumni and their parents now share their post-Montessori school experiences more freely, because it's just a click/send away. For some past students, their time in a Montessori school represents 12 years of their life, building a sense of ownership and home that is not forgotten by a mere change of address. In short, these schools commonly receive letters. The following is from a parent, a forwarding of an e-mail the parent had received from a high school teacher of a Montessori graduate:

"I just wanted to let you know your son ended the semester with one of the only A+ with Honors I have ever given. On that note while I know you know how talented he is, I want to throw in my 2 cents that he should take as many AP classes as possible next year. I have tried hard to keep him challenged in my class, but he is so far beyond other students that I don't think regular classes are the place for him."

Truthfully, this is not uncommon for Montessori graduates, but the parent highlighted the second part of the teacher's e-mail as being more meaningful:

"The other thing I think is great about your son is that even though he finishes his work easily he helps other students. There is one student in particular that sits next to him and she struggles every day. With the patience of a teacher he helps her ALL class. Sometimes I think she is going to wear on his patience but he just gently answers her questions."

Can kindness, in fact, be taught? As Montessorians, we would answer, "No more than we 'teach' geography or arithmetic or science." Rather, a Montessori school creates an environment, carves a space, and maintains a culture that allows a natural process to take place. And while it is not quantified on any conference report, the grace and courtesy aspect of our curriculum is an integral component of the fabric of our classrooms. This serves, strongly, as the tapestry on which our lessons are woven. It is so present, in fact, that a consistent comment I hear from prospective parents, even after a mere 20-minute observation, is the kindness they witness amongst our students, regardless of class level. Most Montessori teachers will relate similar comments from docents, waiters, park rangers, or other adults encountered on field trips.

One time, after an especially moving observation, a prospective parent sat with me in the hallway, asking me the hows and whys of our school. This parent enthusiastically embraced the peacefulness and kindness she saw that morning. "Does that happen every day?," she asked, perhaps a little suspicious. At that precise moment, two 3-year-olds walked by, hand in hand, on their way to deliver a note to the office. "Yeah," I said, "Pretty much."

Imagination

When Montessorians meet for drinks at Montessori bars (they exist, you just need to know the location and password), a topic of interest is sometimes the role of imagination in Montessori environments. Dr. Montessori's view on the subject has led to much discussion, along with some measure of controversy and a large amount of misconception. Maria Montessori's view of imagination stems from her observations of children in the first plane of development (birth to 6 years old) and their attempts at making sense of the world. She referred to children in these early years as having a sensitivity to order. Montessori felt that during these early years, it was best not to confuse a child of 2 or 3 years with fantastic tales of supernatural beings and abilities. One of the most important works of the young child is to define physical reality, the nature of the world, and how things work. She felt, and rightly so, that there was enough miracle present in nature, enough tales of courage in history, and enough intrigue to stir the soul in literature (she was especially fond of Daniel Defoe's *Robinson Crusoe*) to ignite any child's imagination. Simply stated, Montessori felt that it was not appropriate to introduce "fairy tales" until a child had a firm grasp on reality. Unfortunately, this led to the misconception that Montessori somehow discouraged imaginative play. One of the great and emergent powers of a child in the second plane of development (6 to 12 years of age) is the power of imagination. Gone is the child's interest in the sensorial materials. The ability to absorb knowledge is somewhat diminished as well. A 7-year-old is still driven to explore the world, but rather than using the senses as a 3-year-old would, the Elementary-age child is increasingly using his or her mind. In Primary classrooms, children touch and manipulate physical things. In Elementary classrooms, they manipulate mental imagery as part of the learning process. Exploration by thought replaces exploration by mouth. "What?" may be replaced by "How?," and "Where?" may be replaced by "Why?" Because the students have now developed a clearer understanding of the nature of reality AND the role of fantasy, the Montessori teacher seeks to utilize the children's burgeoning imaginations in the study of culture.

My use of the word "imagination" here requires some elucidation. The Montessori definition refers not to the "fairy tale" connotation but to the ability of the Elementary-age child (6 to 12 years old) to move mentally beyond space and time. In a younger child, the mental outlook is one of either Now or Not Now, or Here or Not Here. The older child, however, can imagine what life was like in ancient times and ancient lands. Imagination is the power to "see" that which is not physically present. And subsequent to that imaginative process emerge questions, which fuel enthusiasm, which in turn powers learning. Imagination allows the elementary child to grasp concepts that are too abstract for his or her younger sibling. By studying the attributes of the one, imagination allows the child to generalize about the many. By dissecting a single flower, discovering its stamen and pistil, feeling its delicate petals, the child understands that these parts are present in every flower. Upon hearing that the stars are as myriad as the sands, the child understands the vastness of the cosmos. Such is the power of imagination. Much of the fodder for the cultural curriculum of the Elementary program involves the study of history, culture, and ancient civilizations. For a younger child, anything that happened in the past is "yesterday," and anything that will happen in the future is "tomorrow." But the elementary child has developed a sense of time and the power of imagination, which allow him or her to envision and relate to events and people that occurred in another place and in another time. The value of the impressionistic lesson is clear here, as it allows children to imagine living in an ancient civilization and appreciating the universal needs and tendencies that link them to bygone children across time and space. This development continues into the third plane of development, in the Junior Class, as young adults take on adult roles, in microeconomies and internships, and begin to see themselves as they will be in little more than a few years.

In general terms, there are three types of imagination. Reproductive imagination allows for the recall of that which we have seen before. This is the imagination most utilized in the first plane of development. During the second plane, children develop a creative imagination, the ability to manipulate and combine images and metaphors to better understand abstract concepts. Lastly, children develop an inventive imagination. Now they can visualize that which has yet to come to pass. This is the force that powers initiative, invention, change, development, and the betterment of our world.

These developing powers are manifested at each age level in a Montessori prepared environment. In the Primary classroom, an early emphasis is placed on the sensorial materials. The sensorial materials allow the child to discriminate between objects based on a sensorial quality, such as size and shape. The Pink Tower, the Knobbed Cylinders, the Color Tablets, and the Bells are but a few of the manipulative materials that 3- to 6-year-olds use to organize their perception of the world. The use of reproductive imagination enables children of this age to recall images from previous work and to lay out the Pink Tower cubes in sequence, or place the Bells in order by tone, the Knobbed Cylinders by circumference and depth, and so on. The Lower or Upper Elementary child possesses a creative imagination. This newly acquired power enables the presentation of such abstract concepts as a decimal fraction, or a cosmic tale of creation, or the fundamental needs of ancient cultures. In arithmetic, for instance, the child no longer needs to hold a thousand-cube in his or her hand to imagine such a large quantity. The written numeral 1,000 serves the same purpose. The child begins to work without materials. Entry into the Junior Class marks entry into early adolescence. While students at this age retain a reproductive and creative imagination, this age marks the emergence of the inventive imagination. The Junior Class curriculum challenges students to take abstract concepts learned in one area and apply them in an entirely new way. How are the politics of the American Revolution relevant today? How does one apply an algebraic formula to a new problem? How does a Shakespearean play resonate in popular culture?

The child develops from birth to adolescence in myriad ways, amongst them the development of imagination. A Montessori pedagogy, ever following the child, provides prepared environments and activities that meet the child and the imagination.

Going Out

Lord Alfred Whitehead, an English educator and philosopher and a contemporary of Montessori, remarked that effective education involves an initial introduction to a subject, then a detailed study, and then a return to the material, but now in a much more profound manner. We stroll through a forest, then learn about trees, and then notice how much more meaningful a revisit to the same forest becomes. This mirrors the three-period lesson in Montessori, and I mention it here because we see this play out continually throughout the school year, as children embark on September camping trips, October apple-gathering trips, a myriad of small group outings, or larger trips for older students, to Washington, DC, or even London. On those trips one often witnesses countless children from other schools wandering aimlessly from exhibit to exhibit, while Montessori children find connections to their studies in countless ways. Trips have limited value without this element. It is provided by the faculty, but the children themselves are the ones who must ultimately respond, experience, process, connect, enjoy, and find meaning. And that does not even include the value of working out who is going in which car, working together to maintain the campfire, coming up with a shower schedule, or finding the best way from South Kensington to Twickenham.

Of course, "going out" also includes much less extensive travel. Montessori believed that learning and knowledge could not be contained within a classroom's four walls. For the study of trees, a picture is a poor substitute for seeing, touching, and smelling the real thing. Likewise, field trips to apple orchards are opportunities for teamwork, the practical life of travel, the sheer joy of being 6 years old and taking a bite of a freshly picked apple, and the collection of fruit to be brought back to school for baking and saucing, but also for fraction studies. Studies of water samples are much more meaningful when you are the one that did the collecting.

Going out, whether across the playground, across the town, or across the ocean, is an integral component of a Montessori classroom. It encompasses practical life skills as well as a real-life application of the subject being studied. Ultimately, it is greater than the sum of its parts, and just another thread in the greater tapestry of a Montessori education.

Montessori and the Scouting Movement

Robert Stephenson Smyth Baden-Powell was an English writer and military man who lived from the mid-19th to mid-20th century. Lord Baden-Powell is most well known as the founder of the Scouting movement, the genesis of the Boy Scouts Association both in the United

States and worldwide. But he was also a contemporary of Maria Montessori, and by all accounts, they were mutual admirers.

> *"Dear Dr. Montessori, I have heard with great interest*
> *your commendation of the principles of the Boy Scout Movement*
> *and how you have borne them in mind in devising your scheme*
> *for the education of children below the Scout Wolf Cub age*
> *and mentality. I am very glad to hear that the experiment is*
> *proving successful. ...The cubs have proved successful as Patrol*
> *Leaders and thus have confirmed my feeling that you*
> *can scarcely start too early the training in responsibility and*
> *leadership as an important step in formation of character.*
> *Yours sincerely, Robert Baden-Powell."*

For her part, Montessori pursued an interest in "integrating the Scout training and my own educational system. Children must have social experiences out of doors as well as in the classroom. Scouting fills an empty place in education and supplies a need of great human importance."

Valorization

The thank-you card from the recent graduate was tucked into the striped bag, the words more valuable than the gift. A struggling academic student, she had found a measure of success outside in the school gardens. "Thanks for making me feel confident every time I see the farm (even though I might not have the greenest of thumbs), and making me think, 'there's a little bit of me in that garden, in that shed.' Thanks for making me feel that I helped."

A Montessori environment is carefully prepared to allow children to work to their potential and to move successfully through the planes of development from birth to adulthood. For the first two 6-year planes (Toddler through Upper Elementary), Montessori used the term "normalization" to describe the child's acquisition of developmental characteristics, such as profound spontaneous concentration, an attachment to reality, the power to choose work independently, and a love of silence, order, and work.

During the third plane of development, however, Montessori spoke of a new goal for this new, older child. "Valorization" describes the process an adolescent must go through in order to integrate a mature identity and the sense of being able to succeed in life by his/her own efforts or, in other words, to become an adult. This manifests itself in qualities such as selflessness (believe it or not), confidence, dignity, initiative, independence, helpfulness, good judgement, and the ability to work with others.

The prepared environment of the Junior Class reflects this goal, in part through a component of the curriculum that Montessori named "Occupations." Juniors often operate a series of microeconomies, i.e., student-run small businesses with adult guidance. These economies take the form of products, services, workshops, etc. The wider community supports these efforts through its patronage, while providing a critical learning opportunity for this age group. The early adolescent student learns that he or she is capable of great things and that one can, through effort and in concert with peers, accomplish a real task, complete a real job, prepare and serve a hot lunch to a 6-year-old (and clean the kitchen afterward), plant and harvest a crop, or build a raised bed. These students learn what it means to make a good judgement, the consequences of making a bad one, and the restitution or redress that those choices require of them. The process of valorization is not limited to the farm or the kitchen. The ability to assemble a raised bed parallels the confidence needed to graph a linear equation, to take on a role in Shakespeare, to present oneself at an interview, and to construct one's own future.

Socialization

In one of Maria Montessori's first classrooms in Italy, a shelf intended to hold the school's glassware was loose, and only with great care were the vases and tumblers taken and replaced without the shelf falling to the floor. Legend has it that by the time the carpenter appeared to repair the faulty bracket, the children had developed the requisite careful movements to avoid a crashing of glass, thus rendering the repair unnecessary. Instead of eliminating use of the shelf altogether, or replacing the glass with paper or plastic, time was taken to embrace the situation as an opportunity to learn rather than a situation to avoid.

A response we see time and again to difficult or even potentially difficult situations in traditional schools is to eliminate the activity altogether. Is there the possibility that a child may get cut with a kitchen knife? Then eliminate every cooking activity that requires chopping. Will a family be offended at the inclusion of any religious study or performance? Then eliminate any and all such presentations. Do social interactions hold the possibility of antisocial behavior? Then severely limit the amount of time children spend in social situations.

The Montessori pedagogy takes the opposite approach. Show a child how to use a knife (or any tool) properly, and you give him or her the means and experience to learn its proper use. Include all religions in your cultural studies or school performances, and you give the child full access to the breadth and wonder of humanity's spiritual expression. And rather than minimizing the amount of social time in a child's day, make it an integral part of the day. To do less is a disservice, lest we create a generation of kids who do not know how to socialize or deal with each other.

Socialization at all levels is seen as another strong component of a child's education. The ability to navigate through a classroom of peers, working on a variety of activities with a plentitude of materials, both literally and metaphorically, is well worth the child's concentration and the teacher's support. The prepared environment requires that students engage with each other, in friendship and in conflict, with peers who are alike and different, on an almost minute-to-minute basis. They are the stronger for it. They face the "real world" not handicapped by a lack of practiced social skill but, rather, well prepared, understanding, and adept.

Sharing

A child sits at a small table, intent on the work at hand, focused and in deep concentration, carefully pouring water into small glasses. A second child arrives on the scene and indicates to the adult that he or she also wants to use the material. How does the adult respond? Should the working child be asked to share? Parents and teachers often face the same experiences at home and in the classroom, and sharing is an issue fraught with emotion. Is my child sharing enough? How much should I encourage (perhaps force?) my child to share? Is resistance to sharing a sign of moral failure on the part of my child? On my part? For parents, it is a subject that may come up with their children's friends during a playdate, at the playground, or every night in the living room between siblings. For a Montessori teacher, the issue of sharing comes up daily, at all levels. So how does the above scenario work itself out in the classroom? Are there fights over the one Broad Stair in a Primary classroom? Over the few Bead Frames in a

Lower Elementary classroom? The answer depends largely on the developmental stage of the child. As Montessori observed and legions of child psychologists have confirmed, when children under the age of 6 (Toddler and Primary classrooms) are involved in engaging work appropriate to their developmental stage, they are less concerned about possessiveness. It is only when the available choices are bereft of interest that children exhibit a desire to "own" things. A Montessori prepared environment is full of manipulative, hands-on materials that have called to children for over a hundred years, and the options give a child at any given time ample opportunity to find engaging work. The roles of the teacher are to observe the child and present those materials that are appropriate and, once a material is chosen, to assure the child that he or she has the right to work on it until it is completed, without interruption or sharing. When this limit is part of the fabric of a learning community, it greatly ameliorates friction over sharing. A child can choose to share if he or she wishes… "do you want to build the Pink Tower with me?" …or not. Then the act of sharing is meaningful, voluntary, and not coerced by an adult. A child under the age of 6 years, that is, in the first plane of development (according to Montessori pedagogy), is egocentric and less interested in sharing or being shared with. In the second plane of development (6 to 12 years of age), children are much more social and far more interested in peers than in things, and they are far more engaged in sharing as a social exercise.

Giving

I mentioned to two prospective parents that one of our classes volunteers at the Common Table, a free lunch program in downtown Portsmouth, NH. "We go every

Thursday, and have become an integral part of the volunteer staff," I said. One of the observers, the father of a third grader, shook his head ruefully and remarked, "Huh. At my son's school there is only one 'Caring Day' a year. It's right before the holidays, so everyone feels good about themselves!" I had just returned from our weekly trip and had witnessed children confidently help to serve about 150 free meals and then clean up afterwards. It was easy to see that rather than having a singular experience in caring for others, these young men and women had truly internalized the concept of service. On the ride back to school, one of the eighth graders told a seventh grader, "You're lucky. You still get to do this for all of next year." It would be difficult, nigh on impossible, to tease out all the sources of such a natural grace and caring attitude, but they surely include supportive home environments, good parenting, and positive experiences with helping others grow. In addition, though, on walking around a Montessori school on any given day, you can quickly ascertain that the school is a strong contributor to this empathetic ethos.

I believe that its genesis starts in small ways. Two Primary children were making their way to the office yesterday, and I was addressing three or four prospective parents on a tour. "Excuse us, please," they piped up, and the admiring adults parted to give them passage. It's at moments like these, and they happen often, that I am looked at slightly suspiciously, as if I put these children up to being especially impressive for the sake of the tour. A child in Lower Elementary upsets her Stamp Game as she maneuvers towards a work mat, spilling dozens of wooden stamps on the floor. Without hesitation or prompting from any teacher, small helping hands surround her and begin to scoop and sort the small tiles back into their compartments. Is it any wonder that these young children will later view service at a soup kitchen as a natural extension of what they feel compelled to share of themselves?

Dr. Montessori often proposed that lasting peace in the world will be achieved only when education and peace are seen as necessary parts of each other. A Montessori community takes that responsibility to heart, from the heart.

CHAPTER SIX
A (BRIEF) HISTORY OF MONTESSORI

The word "Montessori" refers to Dr. Maria Montessori, an Italian doctor born in the late 19th century. Using scientific methods to observe and analyze how children learn, she discovered that children's learning capabilities are specific to their developmental stage of life. Montessori saw that young children are capable of long periods of concentration and use learning materials repeatedly. She devised sets of sequenced learning materials that guide children towards reading, writing, understanding place value in mathematics, recognizing geometrical shapes, and having a geographical recognition of the continents and nations. Later, Dr. Montessori recognized the unique learning capabilities of elementary and early adolescent students. Elementary students seek answers to large questions about the universe, their place in it, the human purpose, and issues of social justice. Montessori created an integrated curriculum incorporating anthropology, astronomy, biology, chemistry, geology, geometry, history, literature, mathematics, and zoology. These studies continue into the older years, as young adolescents, who are now ready for higher-order critical thinking, use primary source materials to explore integrated themes drawn from history, philosophy, and science. Dr. Montessori devoted her life to the education and understanding of children. She believed that the purpose of education was to assist in the process of life. The opening of Dr. Montessori's first school, Casa dei Bambini (Children's House), was in Rome, in 1907. Currently, there are over 22,000 Montessori schools worldwide, in 110 countries.

Maria Montessori was born in 1870, in Chiaravalle, Italy. Her father was a financial manager, and her mother was well educated and well read. Early in her childhood, the family moved to Rome, where the young Maria would have experienced the many libraries and museums there. By all accounts, she was an outstanding student and was supported in her academic pursuits by her parents. Despite the cultural barriers she faced as a young woman in the 19th century, she persevered. At age 13, with the goal of becoming an engineer, she was accepted into a previously all-boys technical school. Montessori later changed her focus to medicine and decided to pursue entry into medical school. Her initial application to the University of Rome program was rejected, but she took outside courses, studied diligently, reapplied, and was accepted. There are many accounts detailing some of the trials and prejudices Montessori faced during her matriculation. For example, it was considered indecorous for a woman to be present during the autopsy of a naked male corpse. She was therefore required to do her coursework alone in the morgue, at night. In her memoirs, Montessori recounts that several times the lights were turned off by fellow students, leaving her in the dark!

When she graduated in 1896, Montessori became one of the first female physicians in Italy. After a series of appointments at various hospitals in Rome, Dr.

Montessori's interests and avocation turned towards psychiatry, and she joined a research program that brought her to various asylums across Italy. Focusing on children, she devoted herself to studies of special and regular education. She translated the works of Jean Marc Gaspard Itard (who had gained renown with his work with the "wild boy of Aveyron") and Edouard Seguin, both of whom were critical of the regimented structure of traditional schools at the time, into Italian. The former had developed a few materials for the teaching of the senses, while the latter, his student, had developed a math material that bears his name: the Seguin Board.

Dr. Montessori's work with children in the asylums of Rome did not escape notice, and she was asked to address the National Medical Congress in Turin. She was only 28 years old. In this address, she expounded on her idea that the "delinquency" of the children was a direct result of their appalling lack of nutrition and care, a somewhat controversial view in 1898. Soon after, Montessori became involved with Italy's National League for the Education of Retarded Children and codirected a new school for children with a wide spectrum of disorders. It was here, in a combined school and teacher education center, that Montessori was given the opportunity to observe her theories in action and to refine the use of her pedagogical manipulative materials. The idea that education could be a tool for social progress was galvanized, and her life's pursuit became one of education and not medicine. Three years later, in 1901, Montessori left the school and took a position as a lecturer at the Pedagogic School, a college of the University of Rome.

Coincidental to her emergence as a well-known speaker, educator, and advocate for children's and women's rights, the real estate market in Rome had become tumultuous. Property speculation was rampant, and large apartment complexes were built but left unoccupied, leading to squatters and their children living in abject squalor. Eventually, a group of wealthy businessmen, after restoring one of these developments, began renting apartments to working families, but the unsupervised children of the renters began damaging the property and wreaking havoc. Knowing of Montessori's interest in education and social philosophy, the businessmen sought her out to start a school for them on the apartment grounds. She, in turn, was eager to observe her methods and materials in use beyond the realm of special education and with the general population. On January 6th, 1907, the first Casa dei Bambini, or Children's House, opened, and the world's first Montessori school was now established. On the occasion of opening her first school, in a remark of understated prescience, Montessori wrote, "I had a strange feeling which made me announce emphatically that here was the opening of an undertaking of which the whole world would one day speak."

The days and months that followed were times of great revelation to Montessori, as she introduced a variety of learning activities and observed the children at their work. She came to the inevitable conclusion that children were engaged the most with, and learned the most from, those manipulative materials that were especially designed for their developmental stage. Moreover, she saw that this drive to "autoeducate" was natural and that the role of the teacher was one of guidance and facilitation rather than direct instruction. It is difficult in the early 21st century to fully appreciate just how revolutionary this view of children's education was in the early 20th century. And perhaps it is equally remarkable that the pedagogy spread so quickly and so far. Within a year and a half, there were five schools operating in Rome and Milan. Areas of Switzerland had converted their kindergartens to Montessori environments. By the summer of 1909, 100 student teachers had enrolled in the first-ever Montessori teacher training course, and those lectures, in turn, served as the source material for the classic book *The Montessori Method*. Within 3 years, this book had been translated into 20 languages and had reached number two on the U.S. nonfiction bestseller list. The following decade saw unprecedented growth of the Montessori movement worldwide. Dr. Montessori found it necessary to give up all other commitments and to concentrate on lectures and speaking engagements worldwide. While World War I disrupted plans and slowed its growth, the Montessori method had now gained prominence within the global educational community, and Maria Montessori was an established leader in the field. The rise of Fascism in her native Italy provided the next challenge for Dr. Montessori, limiting her movement. With the signing of the Treaty of Versailles, however, in June 1919, World War I was brought to a close, and Montessori could once again travel and lecture to increasingly supportive audiences in Europe and America. Dr. Montessori based herself in Barcelona, along with her son, Mario, and eventually four grandchildren: Mario, Jr., Rolando, Marilena, and Renilde. There is some historical debate on her son Mario's paternity, as his mother never revealed the identity of his father. Most believe that Guiseppe Montesano, the director of one of the early schools where Montessori studied before she opened her own, was Mario's father. In any case, the boy was raised outside of Rome, and while Montessori visited him often, he did not know her as his mother until he was much older.

Dr. Montessori's development of a permanent center for teacher education in the Montessori method gained focus throughout the 1920s, yet it was impossible to achieve with the rise of Fascism in Spain, Germany, and her native Italy. By 1933, Montessori schools were banned in Berlin, and Montessori's books were burned along with her effigy. In earlier years, Benito Mussolini was more than willing to tout Montessori's work as a symbol of Italy and of Fascism. A few years later, however, Mussolini's plans to incorporate Montessori's schools with his youth movement were running counter to Maria's vision of peace education. The outbreak of the Spanish Civil War forced the family to flee to England and then to the Netherlands.

In 1939, Maria and her son embarked on a training course and lecture tour to India. With the outbreak of the war, and because of their status as Italian citizens, Mario was interned and Maria placed under house arrest. What was to be a 3-month stay turned into 7 years. Maria spent the time in the small rural village of Kodaikanal, and she gained release for Mario 1 year after, on her 70th birthday, following a request to the Indian government. It was here that she and Mario developed much of the Montessori Elementary program, including the theme of Cosmic Education, the guiding overarching theme of her pedagogy for ages 6 to 12. Her experience in India not only greatly influenced her own thinking but also affected many others, as she trained thousands of teachers in the course of her time there, a legacy seen in India to this day.

With the cessation of World War II, Dr. Montessori returned to Europe, settling in the Netherlands in 1946 and reuniting with her grandchildren. A year later, at the age of 77, she addressed the United Nations Educational, Scientific and Cultural Organization (UNESCO). The topic was "Education and Peace," a theme that had become her passion for the last decade of her life. This led to her nomination for a Nobel Peace Prize in 1949, the first of three nominations she would receive (1949, 1950, and 1951). In 1951, Montessori gave her last public lecture, at the Ninth Annual Montessori Congress in London. She passed away on May 6th, 1952, in the Netherlands, with her son Mario by her bedside.

Educational historians usually refer to two significant growth periods for the Montessori method in the United States, separated by nearly 40 years. The first surge came in the early 1900s, when a hundred Montessori schools opened across America in a span of 5 years. In 1915, at the Panama Pacific International Exposition at the San Francisco World's Fair, a fully functional glass Montessori prepared environment was exhibited. It contained a class of children of 3 to 6 years of age and operated as an artificial classroom for the Fair's 4-month duration. Thousands of children applied to be a student in the classroom and, presumably, to be gawked at. That they be new to any school experience was Montessori's only requirement. The country had been shown a new educational paradigm, and the Montessori method flourished, only to decline precipitously over the next decade. Early media reports sensationalized the Montessori method as a near-miracle method that could teach 2-year-olds to read. Alternately, they grossly misrepresented basic tenets of her work. The *New York Tribune* breathlessly exclaimed, "Smash Your Toys If You Want To. Dr. Montessori Gives Children Leeway to Wreck Christmas Presents. Mothers Alone to Blame, She Says. They Don't Pick Gifts that Appeal to Infantile Mind, Woman Teacher Asserts." It would be 4 decades before Montessori experienced similar growth, but this time it would be stronger and enduring. Unfortunately, it was a resurgence that Montessori did not live to see.

With her death in 1952, the question of what the future held for her eponymous pedagogy was in question. While Montessori schools were prevalent in Europe and India, they had been marginalized in America after their initial, short-lived success in the 1920s. The subsequent growth of Montessori education in the United States is largely credited to a woman named Nancy McCormick Rambusch. In 1953, Rambusch traveled to Europe and attended the Tenth International Montessori Conference. There she met Mario Montessori, Maria's son and successor as head of AMI (Association Montessori Internationale). At his urging, she returned to New York City and began giving Montessori lessons in her apartment to her own children, as well as those of a few friends. By 1958, with the support of some prominent Connecticut families, she opened the Whitby School in Greenwich. This is generally recognized as the first Montessori school in America, or at least the first successful and long-lasting one. Rambusch stayed in close contact with Mario, and in 1960, she was appointed the U.S. representative of AMI. The nascent movement was greatly bolstered by favorable publicity in publications such as *Time*, *Newsweek*, *The Saturday Evening Post*, and *The New York Times*. Parent interest grew exponentially.

Rambusch wanted to increase the stature of Montessori teacher education programs, and to that end, she instituted the requirement of a bachelor's degree as a prerequisite for admittance. She also sought to broaden the curriculum requirements for student teachers. These changes, among others, created a rift between herself and Mario, and in 1963, the American Montessori Society (AMS) officially split from AMI.

Today, AMS is the largest accrediting organization of Montessori teachers, schools, and teacher education courses in the world. There are more Montessori schools in the United States, some 4,500, than in any other country. Over 100 teacher education courses offer certification, and Montessori education continues to make inroads into public schools. There are over 400 Montessori public school programs in the United States, most of which are charter schools. Arizona, California, Florida, Michigan, Ohio, and South Carolina boast the largest numbers of public Montessori schools, with the last offering a "Montessori" designation to graduates on their state certification.

AMS is a nonprofit organization and is dedicated to encouraging and supporting the use of the Montessori teaching approach in private and public schools. The organization is member supported, with its funding coming mainly from Montessori-credentialed teachers, schools, administrators, teacher education programs, and parents of Montessori schoolchildren. At present, AMS is 10,000 members strong and is committed to furthering Montessori philosophy, making it a growing educational alternative, and promoting better education for all children. Its mission statement states that "AMS provides the leadership and inspiration to make Montessori a significant voice in education. The Society advocates quality Montessori education, strengthens members through its services, and champions Montessori principles to the greater community." AMS also accredits Montessori teacher education courses, which are equivalent in time and scope to a master's program. In fact, several universities offer a Montessori credential in conjunction with a master's degree. Teachers are credentialed within the same parameters as the environments: Infant/Toddler, Early Childhood (3- to 6-year-olds), Elementary I (6- to 9-year-olds), Elementary II (9- to 12-year-olds), and Secondary.

AMI is the original organizing body of Montessori education. Formed in 1929 by Maria and Mario Montessori, it is the largest credentialing organization internationally. It seeks to fulfill its mission, "to support the natural development of the human being from birth to maturity, enabling children to become the transforming elements of society, leading to a harmonious and peaceful world." AMI is located in Amsterdam, with affiliate associations in many countries, and is involved in the accreditation of schools and training centers and the education of teacher trainers, as well as in providing publications, seminars, conferences, and consulting services. AMI's school recognition program provides certificates to schools that meet its standards at three different levels: recognition, affiliation, and association. In the United States, AMI is represented by AMI-USA and NAMTA (the North American Montessori Teachers' Association).

Regardless of affiliation, Montessori teacher training courses draw adult teachers from a wide variety of backgrounds. These individuals range from education majors to former business people embarking on a second career to, not uncommonly, parents of children attending Montessori schools. Their commonality dwarfs their differences. They are largely inquisitive, hard-working, and dedicated, which is either a cause or result of their choice to pursue a Montessori credential. This credential will take the larger part of 2 years to attain, and even then it will be valid for only one 3-year age span. Some summers ago I was in Charleston, SC, teaching Montessori philosophy, methods, and Lower Elementary mathematics to a group of aspiring teachers. South Carolina has become a hotbed for Montessori these days, and it is expanding into public schools there as rapidly as it is in the private sector. In this particular group, there were seasoned teachers from traditional schools, Montessori Primary teachers, and one Montessori Upper Elementary teacher, all of whom were spending a large chunk of their summer learning the Lower Elementary curriculum. Near the end of the week, I was showing some "exponent and powers" lessons, and I had a series of squares and cubes arrayed on a mat in front of me, with the beauty of the mathematical patterns clearly evident. One of the Primary teachers noted, "Those 10 cubes are the same sizes as the pink cube in a Primary classroom." The Upper Elementary teacher remarked, "In Upper Elementary we use it for cubing and volume work." There was a long, thoughtful pause from the group, and then one of the youngest of the group, a woman who was just out of college, said, almost to herself, "Wow. I think I'm going to like this…"

CHAPTER SEVEN
MONTESSORI AT HOME AND IN SOCIETY

Montessori in the Home

Parents of children attending a Montessori school are naturally interested in extending this developmental style of learning into the home. This has given rise to a full-blown cottage industry offering parents everything from specifications for hand sawing their own thousand-cubes to in-home consultations (step one: "observing the family dynamics"), thus ranging from the practical to the downright creepy. Parents who desire to introduce an increased consistency to their child-rearing without necessarily donning safety goggles or inviting strangers to comment on their tone at the dinner table can keep a few things in mind. In reality, it takes very little to implement some key aspects of a Montessori education in the home. As a parent and teacher, I have always found that good parenting and good teaching constantly overlap. Common sense rules at home and in the classroom.

A strong component of any Montessori classroom is the support it gives towards a child's independence. From a Toddler student putting on his or her own shoes to a Primary-age child making a snack, an Elementary-age child checking his or her own math problems, or a Junior student running his or her own business, our classrooms encourage the child's efforts towards autonomy. There are several ways of introducing this element at home. To support a child's ability to dress unassisted, one can set up easily accessed crates (one for socks, one for shirts, etc.) that allow the child to choose an outfit. While you may cringe at some of the combinations the child comes up with, the lesson is well worth it. Similar efforts can be made to allow children to get their own snacks, make their own lunches, or choose what they want for breakfast (for instance, pictures of pancakes, cereal, etc., can be put in envelopes marked by day). The practical life shelves in a Toddler classroom hold buttoning and zippering frames, pouring and pincer-grip activities, and food preparation items. The tools used are child-sized but are not toys, and they allow children to do the same types of work that they see their parents or older siblings perform. For the home, similar tools can be purchased or adapted (for instance, sawing off some of the handle end of a rake).

Another strong attribute of a Montessori environment is that it allows children to learn new concepts and to exercise new skills by using real-life situations. Projects around the house lend themselves to your child's involvement, regardless of his or her age. Measuring, marking, cutting, and nailing can all be adapted as needed (the adult pounds in the nail past the possibility of bending, or pre-drills holes for easy screwing). Meal preparation is a great way to continue the practical life and math activities that come with measuring and mixing ingredients. Gardening is perhaps the most obvious opportunity available during the short growing season in New England. This is another experience that is easily adaptable for a wide age span.

Finally, employing an element of choice in your parenting will dovetail nicely with the work at school. While the child relies on you to set the parameters for behavior and safety, giving the child freedom within a structure is an excellent vehicle for development. In this way, "Montessori in the Home" is just a realization that the concepts of nurturing independence and awareness of the natural world and providing open-ended activities are just as valuable in the home as they are at school.

"The Montessori Mafia"

A strange title, isn't it? While the *Wall Street Journal's* choice for a headline is questionable, the accompanying editorial by Peter Sims is not; in his article, Sims extols the virtues of a Montessori education, specifically as preparation for some of the leading creative business leaders. Sims states, "The Montessori educational approach might be the surest route to joining the creative elite, which are so over represented by school's alumni that one might suspect a Montessori Mafia: Google's founders Larry Page and Sergei Brin, Amazon's Jeff Bezos, videogame pioneer Will Wright, and Wikipedia founder Jimmy Wales, not to mention Julia Child and Sean 'P.Diddy' Combs."

An extensive 6-year study about the way creative business executives think was undertaken by Brigham Young University and INSEAD (a global business school). It surveyed 3,000 executives and interviewed 500 people who had either started innovative companies or invented new products. The article quotes the head of the study: "A number of the innovative entrepreneurs also went to Montessori schools, where they learned to follow their curiosity."

A 2006 study published in *Science* compared the educational achievements of low-income students in

Milwaukee who attended Montessori schools with those of children enrolled in other preschools, by lottery. "By the end of kindergarten," the article quotes, "Montessori students proved to be significantly better prepared for elementary school in reading and math skills than the non-Montessori students. They also tested better on executive function (the ability to adapt to changing and more complex problems), an indicator of future and life success."

In his editorial, Sims concluded, "Perhaps it's just a coincidence that Montessori alumni lead two of the world's most innovative companies. Or perhaps the Montessori Mafia can provide lessons for us all even though it's too late for most of us to attend Montessori. We can change the way we've been trained to think. That begins in small achievable ways, with increased experimentation and inquisitiveness. Those who work with Mr. Bezos, for example, find his ability to ask 'why not?' or 'what if?' as much as 'why?' to be one of his most advantageous qualities. Questions are the new answers."

Montessori without the "M" Word

Recently I traveled to a school district outside of Denver as part of a team of educators working on public school reform for my "home" district in Berwick, Maine. There is a veritable groundswell of interest in this topic these days, and everyone from the Annenberg Foundation to the Nellie Mae Foundation and groups such as RISC (Re-Inventing Schools Coalition) is providing both input and grant money to further the agenda of moving traditional public schools out of a 70-year rut.

What struck me as I read books with titles such as *Delivering on the Promise—The Education Revolution* and handouts such as "Defining Student Centered Learning" and "What are the 21st Century Skills Students Need?" was how similar the components of this "new" approach to education were to a traditional Montessori pedagogy. Consider the following from one such "coalition of corporations and organizations that serves as a catalyst to position 21st century skills at the center of U.S. K-12 education by building collaborative partnerships among education, business, communities, and government" (I can only imagine how long it took a committee to come up with THAT mission statement):

"Today's (and tomorrow's) market seeks employees who have the skills needed to succeed in work, school, and life. In addition to core content knowledge, this skill set includes the following:

- 21st century content—global awareness, financial, business, and entrepreneurial literacy, and health and wellness awareness
- Learning and thinking skills—critical thinking and problem-solving skills, communication skills, creativity and innovation skills, collaboration skills, contextual learning skills, and information and media literacy skills
- Information and communications technology literacy
- Life skills—leadership, ethics, accountability, adaptability, personal productivity, personal responsibility, people skills, self-direction, and social responsibility"

I see these very qualities developed every day in Montessori schools, but the biggest frustration in professional Montessori education these days is in marketing the method and bringing it, deservedly, to the much larger public school system. Buzzwords abound: "authentic assessment," "hands-on manipulative materials," "curriculum integration," "peer teaching," etc. Specific Montessori materials notwithstanding, it is interesting how much Montessori pedagogy is only now being recognized as superior. Even without the "m" word.

Validation

One of the many gratifying aspects of being involved with Montessori education, as an educator or parent, is the continued validation on a scientific basis of what we have known intuitively all along. "Maria Montessori really got everything right..." notes Dr. Steve Hughes, Ph.D., who is President of the American Academy of Pediatric Neuropsychology. In his video, "Montessori and the Future of Education," he states, "She anticipated so much of what we know about neuroscience, brain development, and optimum models of education."

Part of any credentialed Montessori teacher's education is a strong component of training in child development, including the stages of development, the characteristics that mark these periods, and the rationale for the scope and sequence of materials available to children at each level. Dr. Hughes realizes, "A skillful Montessori teacher knows what stage a child is in their brain development and they are meeting it, and they are feeding it." In fact, "The Montessori method is like education designed by a pediatric developmental neuropsychologist."

As school districts and educational pundits wrangle over the newest curriculum, the latest reading program, and the budgets needed to support it all, they would be well served to listen to the science behind the pedagogy. Hughes continues, "If we decided that the purpose of education should be to help every child's brain reach its highest developmental potential, we would have to radically rethink school. The task seems insurmountable, yet this work has already been done. In fact, it was done over a hundred years ago. When examined through the lens of environmental enrichment and brain development, Montessori education presents a radically different—and radically effective—educational approach that may be the best method we've got to ensure the optimal cognitive, social, and emotional development of every child."

CHAPTER EIGHT
CONCLUSION

Walking with great care, the young child brought the Stamp Game to the table, gently placed it down, and opened the lid. Smiling shyly at me, she carefully began laying out the first and second addends, in horizontal rows, one under the other, carefully aligning the thousands, hundreds, tens, and units by place value. Could this be a scene from any Lower Elementary classroom at any Montessori school in America? It certainly could be, as this can be observed daily in our schools. In this case, however, the school was Kiara Karitas, and the school was located on the other side of the world, in Jakarta, Indonesia. The girl, Hee Youn, was a first-year student in the Lower Elementary classroom.

A few years back, the larger Montessori community of educators, parents, administrators, and children celebrated the centennial anniversary of the first Montessori school. That milestone spoke to the lasting power of a profound pedagogy that has truly stood the test of time, allowing children to learn to their potential, to gain an insight into knowledge that is both integrated and internalized, and to develop loving hearts and inquiring minds. In my role as a school board member for my local district in southern

Maine, where math curricula, literacy programs, and science textbooks shift with the vagaries of educational reform, I saw firsthand the disadvantages of moving from one Newest Thing to the Next Newest Thing, as well as the expense and learning curve it requires for teachers and children alike. If it comes to pass that you attach the adjective "Montessori" to your label as "parent" or "educator," you will find that the Next Newest Thing has been there along, and it is extraordinary. Perhaps too often we take it for granted. A common experience for most Montessori teachers, while on a field trip or outing, is to hear from a docent or business owner, "Your children are so well behaved." We are usually mildly surprised by the comment. It's not that we doubt their judgement, it is just a matter of expectation. We are with these children for full days and for 3 years, and what "outsiders" see as extraordinary, we see as, well… ordinary. Similarly, about 75 people are brought into most Montessori schools in any given year, many of them parents touring the school. The vast majority of them are seeing a Montessori school for the first time. After their visit and a subsequent observation, a teacher will often catch me in the hall and bemoan the fact that the visitor observed "a crazy morning." The situation is akin to Roger Federer having a bad match: his "bad match" still vastly exceeds our best efforts, and the same applies to the above scenario (the perception is always relative to the expectations and experiences brought to it). Because, invariably, the parent observing, who is getting an initial look at a Montessori environment with fresh eyes (a beginner's mind), will gush about the peace in the room, the kindness of the children, and the attentiveness and respect shown by and given to the adults.

As parents, teachers, or students, we inevitably begin to see the special as simply routine, the exceptional as commonplace, and the miraculous as mundane. The truth is, it is a sublime gift to be together, for all of us: learning, laughing, playing, spilling things, picking them back up, finding our way to circle, or finding our way, period. But what struck me in Jakarta (and Seoul, and Nashville, and Sarasota...) was how the span of Montessori not only reaches back 100 years but also reaches across the world. What does it say of an educational system that it can speak so forcefully, with such profound results, to parents and children in schools from New Hampshire to California to Asia, Africa, Europe, and beyond? What does it say about the Montessori method that it can unite so many schools in a common model, using the same Montessori materials and the same prepared environments? What does it say about this worldwide and historical community of teachers, students, and families, who wear different clothes, write in different languages, and give and receive lessons in different tongues, but are united all the same? I would not have bothered to ask Hee Youn. She was too busy, and wouldn't have cared. And, frankly, my Bahasa is lousy.

FURTHER READING

Visit our website:
http://keystomontessori.com

As an independent author, reviews are critically important in helping others find books like *Follow the Child*. Please consider leaving a review at the retailer where you purchased this paperback.

Made in the USA
Middletown, DE
30 August 2015